the INCREDIBLE JOURNEY *of* FAITH

RAY PRITCHARD

CROSSWAY BOOKS

A MINISTRY OF
GOOD NEWS PUBLISHERS
WHEATON, ILLINOIS

The Incredible Journey of Faith

Adapted and expanded from part of *The Road Best Traveled,* copyright © 1995 by Ray Pritchard. Published by Crossway Books.

Copyright © 2005 by Ray Pritchard

Published by Crossway Books
        a ministry of Good News Publishers
        1300 Crescent Street
        Wheaton, Illinois 60187

Cover design: Jon McGrath

Cover photo: Getty Images

First printing, 2005

Printed in the United States of America

Unless otherwise indicated, Scripture quotations are taken from *Holy Bible: English Standard Version,* copyright © 2001 by Crossway Bibles, a division of Good News Publishers. All rights reserved. Used by permission.

Scriptures indicated as from NIV are taken from *Holy Bible: New International Version®.* Copyright © 1973, 1978, 1984 by International Bible Society. Used by permission of Zondervan Publishing House. All rights reserved. The "NIV" and "New International Version" trademarks are registered in the United States Patent and Trademark Office by International Bible Society. Use of either trademark requires the permission of International Bible Society.

Scriptures indicated as from KJV are taken from the *King James Version.*

Library of Congress Cataloging-in-Publication Data
Pritchard, Ray, 1952-
   The incredible journey of faith / Ray Pritchard.
     p. cm.
   Adapted and expanded from part of The road best traveled. c1995.
   ISBN 1-58134-612-3
   1. Christian life. I. Pritchard, Ray, 1952-   II. Title.
BV4501.3.P765   2004
248.4—dc22   2004023910

ML		13	12	11	10	09	08	07	06	05
15	14	13	12	11	10	9	8	7	6	5	4	3	2	1

To
DR. ALETTA BELL,
veteran missionary to India.
She has lived the incredible journey of faith.

CONTENTS

WITH GRATITUDE

I owe special thanks to my many friends at Crossway Books who make writing a pleasure and publishing a ministry. With special thanks to Lane Dennis, Marvin Padgett, Ted Griffin, Geoff Dennis, Randy Jahns, and Kathy Jacobs. Brian Ondracek had the original vision for this book. I am grateful to the elders, staff, and congregation of Calvary Memorial Church who do so much to encourage me to keep on writing. And to my wife, Marlene, who smiled and said she knew I would finish this book.

INTRODUCTION

This summer my wife, Marlene, and I spent a month on the road. We were in Michigan for a week, then in New York, then back to Oak Park, Illinois, for a few days, then out to California. Before we left, we asked God to speak to us about things he wanted us to know. I've learned that's not a prayer to pray lightly. If you truly want God to speak to you, buckle your seat belt because God always speaks to those who are willing to hear. As we journeyed from place to place, we prayed and watched and listened, and we talked together about what we felt God was saying to us.

We wrote down pages of insights the Lord was giving us. A lot of it came through things we "happened" to hear and conversations in which little pieces of truth were revealed to us. Sometimes it came as insights that seemed to drop from the sky. And we wrote it all down so we could think about it later. Among the many things God showed us, two stand out.

The first is the principle of intentionality. By that I mean, living life on purpose, and not just drifting through one day after another. It's so easy to go through a day, and be very busy, and yet come to the end and say, "What did I do today?" *Busyness is no guarantee that you are actually doing anything important.* Busyness may be a cover for a lack of purpose in your life. Too many times we sit on the banks of the river while the current of life rushes right by us. And then one day we wake up and die. God spoke to Marlene and me very clearly about living intentionally, with purpose—not just filling each day with activity, but finding out what really matters, and then going and doing it.

Not everything matters equally. Some things we spend lots of time on don't really matter at all. But it's easy to let those things clutter up our days. We came back with new resolve to invest our lives in the work of the Kingdom in a new way. We're still thinking and praying and working that out each day. But just the simple resolve to say (with the apostle Paul), "One thing I do" (Philippians 3:13) has made a huge difference for us.

As we continued our travels, God spoke to us about his will. Usually we think of God's will in geographic terms: Should we live in San Diego or Jackson or Baltimore? But the Bible speaks more often in terms of character and spiritual growth. *The Lord impressed on us that who we are is more important than where we are. And what we are on the inside is more important than what we do on the outside.* After all, if you are the right sort of person on the inside, you are more likely to do what God wants on the outside. The heart matters more to God than geography. If we are the right kind of people, then it doesn't matter too much where we happen to live. We can be God's people in San Diego or Jackson or Baltimore. And if we're going to live only for ourselves and ignore God, we can do that in San Diego or Jackson or Baltimore. I don't mean to suggest that geography doesn't matter. It matters greatly, but it's not the determining factor in life.

The life of faith is a journey with God that begins the moment we trust Christ and continues until the moment we die. The title of this book suggests that living by faith is an *incredible* journey, and that is certainly true. More and more I have come to see that life is all about learning to give up control of those things we never really controlled in the first place. That's a hard lesson to learn, and most of us have to learn it over and over again; but when we do, the incredible journey begins. As we move through the chapters of this book, we'll discover various aspects of that incredible journey. We'll trace Abraham's journey to the

Promised Land, and we'll meet a man from Nigeria along the way. Later we'll examine a young man at the crossroads of life, and we'll venture to the rutted roads of Haiti. Eventually we'll travel back in time 2,500 years to watch the Hebrew heroes who refused to bow down to a statue, and we'll travel with Karen Watson as her faith takes her to a city in northern Iraq. The final chapter takes us into a Persian court where a beautiful young woman named Esther decides to lay it all on the line because of her faith.

We will end with the challenge to put our hands in the hand of Almighty God who leads us into the unknown future. Here's the final sentence of the book: *To walk with the Lord is the greatest of all joys, and it is indeed safer than a known way.* That's what the life of faith is all about, and it truly is an incredible journey. If that sounds exciting to you, turn the page and let's get started.

THE INCREDIBLE JOURNEY

It is sometimes said that a crisis never makes a man—it only reveals what he already is. That thought is both comforting and frightening because we all wonder how we would react if everything we held dear was really on the line.

Our family . . .

Our health . . .

Our career . . .

Our future . . .

Our life . . .

We wonder, would we have the faith to make it? Or would we collapse? All the things we say we believe—would they still be enough when the crunch comes?

A chapter in the Bible tells us about men and women whose faith was strong in times of crisis. The names written there are like a biblical hall of fame: Abel . . . Enoch . . . Noah . . . Abraham . . . Sarah . . . Jacob . . . Joseph . . . Moses . . . David. Different people, different stories, widely separated in time and space. Stories that span thousands of years. Stories that encompass murder, natural catastrophe, family treachery, physical weakness, failed dreams, missed opportunities, sibling rivalry, and military conquests. The men and women whose stories are told in this particular chapter differ in every way but one: *What they did, they did by faith.*

So when the crisis came, it did not make them—it only revealed what they already were.

That chapter is Hebrews 11.

THE MAN FROM NIGERIA

Twenty years ago I pastored a church in Garland, Texas, a suburb on the northeast side of Dallas. Because of our location and our unofficial connection with Dallas Theological Seminary, a steady stream of students attended the church. The most unusual seminary student I ever met came to us late one summer. At the time I did not know him or his story. He had traveled from Nigeria with his wife and six children to study at the seminary, hoping someday to return to his homeland to serve as a leader of the New Salem Church. When I met him, Lekan Olatoye was forty-four years old.

I noticed at once that he was very friendly. He and his wife and their children fit right in. In the course of time he helped out around the church. When we discovered he had a knack for things electrical, we put him to work repairing the many broken fixtures in the building we were renting. Later he and Irene taught Sunday school to the toddlers. He signed up to take Evangelism Explosion training. Many Tuesday nights we visited new residents in Garland, inviting them to our church and (whenever we got the chance) sharing the Gospel. I can remember the night Lekan shared his testimony during a visit. He told of coming to Christ out of an animistic background, of a radical conversion experience that completely changed the direction of his life. The precise details escape me, but the image of joy inscribed on his face remains in my mind across the years. That year at Christmastime when Marlene and I had an open house, our friend's whole family came. I can still see all eight of them sitting in a row on a couch in our living room.

A few months later we had a men's retreat at Pine Cove in east Texas. That Friday night Lekan joined in our air-hockey competition. The next morning we had a sports tournament, and he joined right in. He took notes during the morning Bible study. And that afternoon, about 2:15 P.M., I passed him as he was going to the pool, a towel draped casually around his neck. He went swimming and then joined a lazy game of volleyball.

NO MIRACLE THAT DAY

Suddenly he pitched forward and fell to the ground, his glasses flying from his face. The other men thought he had fainted from overexertion, but when they could get no pulse, it was clear that something terrible had happened. A cry for help went out, and a paramedic who was with us administered CPR. Men gathered in groups to pray. At length an ambulance came and took him away.

But there was to be no miracle that day. In truth, he was dead before he hit the ground. It was a stroke or perhaps a massive heart attack.

We gathered our things and went back to Dallas. I have faced many difficult tasks as a pastor, but the hardest thing I have ever done was to tell that sweet wife she no longer had a husband and to tell those dear children they no longer had a father.

I pondered that day—and many days since—what it all meant. A man in the prime of his life leaves his country, his home, and his job and goes overseas to study God's Word. He means to return to his own people someday. His only purpose in going is to fulfill God's will for his life. He has no other motive. At enormous personal sacrifice, he walks away from a lucrative career and takes his family halfway around the world.

Then he is cut down at the age of forty-four before he even gets started.

What does it all mean? Why would God allow such a thing to happen to a man dedicated to doing his will? And in a larger sense, what does such a tragedy teach us about discovering and doing God's will ourselves?

In order to understand the answer to that question, I would like to focus our attention on Hebrews 11. Not on the whole chapter but on one man, Abraham. And not his whole story, but the record of his incredible journey to the Promised Land. The long version of Abraham's life is given in Genesis; the Hebrews passage is the short summary. Hebrews 11:8-10 tells of one man who obeyed God's call at great personal sacrifice. It tells us what he did; more importantly, it tells us why he did it.

A PLACE CALLED UR

Let's begin with some brief facts about Abraham. When we meet him in the Bible, he is living four thousand years ago in a far-off place called Ur of the Chaldees—on the banks of the Euphrates River, not far from the mouth of the Persian Gulf. No doubt he and his wife, Sarah, worship the moon-god Sin. He is a prosperous, middle-aged man, successful by any human standard. Life has been good to Abraham and Sarah. Certainly they have no reason to complain.

It is at precisely this moment that God speaks to him—clearly, definitely, unmistakably. What God says will change his life—and ultimately alter the course of world history.

Truth #1:
Living by faith means accepting God's call
without knowing where it will lead

"By faith Abraham obeyed when he was called to go out to a place that he was to receive as an inheritance. And he went out, not knowing where he was going" (Hebrews 11:8). There is only one way to describe Ur of the Chaldees. It was a world-class city. Archaeologists tell us that in Abraham's day perhaps 250,000 people lived there. It was a center of mathematics, astronomy, commerce, and philosophy. People from outlying areas moved to Ur because they wanted to be part of that great city.

No doubt many of Abraham's friends thought he was crazy. Why would anyone want to leave Ur? Obeying God's call meant giving up his friends, his career, his traditions, his home, his position, his influence, and his country. More than that, it meant risking his health and his future on a vague promise from an unseen God to lead him to "the land that I will show you" (Genesis 12:1).

When Abraham left Ur, he burned his bridges behind him. For him there could be no turning back. Once he left the walls of Ur, he was on his own, following God's call into the unknown.

You say, "He gave all that up?"

Yes.

"That's kind of strange, isn't it?"

Is it?

Please don't miss the point. *When God calls, there are no guarantees about tomorrow (on earth anyway).* Abraham truly didn't know where he was going, didn't know how he would get there, didn't know how long it would take, and didn't even know for sure how he would know he was there when he got there. All he knew was that God had called him. Period. Everything else was up in the air.

You want a long life? So do I.

You want to rise in your profession? So do I.

You want lots of friends? So do I.

You want to grow old and die with your family around you? So do I.

There's nothing wrong with those desires. All of us feel that way. But living by faith means no guarantees and no certainty about the future.

If you truly want to do God's will, sometimes you will find yourself exactly where Abraham was—setting out on a new journey that doesn't seem to make sense from the world's point of view. I feel compelled to mention here the impossibility of being 100 percent certain in advance. Do you think Abraham was 100 percent certain? Not a chance. The only certainty he had was that God had called him and that he must obey. The rest was shrouded in mystery. That fact makes his obedience all the more impressive. Hebrews 11:8 says he "obeyed" and "went." There was no greater miracle in his life than that. Everything else that happened flowed from this basic decision. *God called; he obeyed.* That truth was the secret of his life. He stepped out in faith even though there were no guarantees about his own personal future.

You see a man at 2:15 P.M. and he's fine. By 3 P.M. he's dead.

What does that mean? Was his faith weak? No. Had he sinned? No. Was he somehow out of God's will? No. Did God make a mistake? No. Did God break his promise? No. Did my friend plan to die that day? Absolutely not.

Let me put it another way: *Living by faith means stepping out for God and leaving the results to him.* It's not a guarantee of long life and good success. You may have those blessings. But you may not.

The life of faith means, "I am going to be the man or woman God wants me to be, no matter where it leads. I don't know the future, but I'm trusting him to work out the details. In the meantime, I am stepping out by faith and will follow where he leads me."

That brings us to the second great truth about living by faith.

Truth #2:
Living by faith means waiting on God
to keep his promises

"By faith he went to live in the land of promise, as in a foreign land, living in tents with Isaac and Jacob, heirs with him of the same promise" (Hebrews 11:9). There is within all of us a natural desire to settle down. Several years ago my wife and I were in the process of selling our home and buying another. Even though we were only moving a few miles, the entire experience was traumatic and disruptive. The older I get, the less I like to move. I value coming home to the same place and the same faces every day. Our home was filled with boxes waiting to be transported to our new house. To me, it was unsettling to look at bare walls that only a few days before were covered with familiar pictures. Suddenly that home looked less like a home and more like a building where we used to live in some distant past. And for a time when I drove past our new house it didn't yet register as "home." The whole experience left me with a vague sense of uneasiness, of homelessness if you will.

Multiply that feeling by a factor of 100 and spread it out over fifty years and you approximate Abraham's situation as he came to the Promised Land. Our text tells us that he was "living in tents." I know lots of people who like to camp on vacation, but I don't know anyone who voluntarily lives in a tent as a permanent residence. Tents speak of impermanence, of the possibility of moving on at any moment, of the fact that you live on land you do not personally own.

That's Abraham. He didn't own anything in the Promised Land. God had promised to give him the land; yet he lived like "a stranger in a foreign country" (v. 9, NIV). If you don't own the land, you can't build a permanent dwelling there.

In many ways this is even more remarkable than leaving Ur in the first place. As long as he was traveling across the desert, he could dream about the future. But when he got to Canaan, all illusions disappeared. Think of what he didn't find:

- no "Welcome, Abraham" sign.
- no discount coupons from the merchants.
- no housewarming party.
- no visit from the Welcome Wagon.
- no mayor with the key to the city.
- no band playing "Happy Days Are Here Again."

• no ticker-tape parade.

Nobody expected him. Nobody cared that he had come. Nobody gave him anything.

God had promised him the land . . . but he had to scratch out an existence in tents. Hundreds of years would pass before the promise was completely fulfilled. Abraham never saw it happen. Neither did Isaac or Jacob.

Was Abraham in the will of God? Yes. Was he right to leave Ur? Yes. Was he doing what God wanted him to do? Yes. Why, then, was he living in tents? Because God's timetable is not the same as ours. He's not in a big hurry like we are. God works across the generations to accomplish his purposes; we're worried about which dress or shirt to buy for the big party this weekend. There is a big difference in those two perspectives.

A third principle at work in Abraham's life is the ultimate key to the life of faith.

Truth #3:
Living by faith means never taking your eyes off heaven

"For he was looking forward to the city that has foundations, whose designer and builder is God" (Hebrews 11:10). Abraham looked for a city with foundations—that is, for a "*city*," not a lonely spot in the desert. He wanted to live in a place filled with other people. He also looked for a city with "*foundations*," a place with security and permanence that could not be found in a tent. That meant he was looking for a city designed and built by God. Why? Because all earthly cities eventually crumble to dust.

I have visited the ruins of the ancient city of Jericho. When most people think of Jericho, they think of the city whose walls came tumbling down in the days of Joshua. But that's only *one* Jericho. Archaeologists have discovered *layers* of Jericho, one after another, the city having been built, destroyed, and rebuilt across the centuries. The same is true of Jerusalem. When you visit Old Jerusalem, you aren't exactly walking where Jesus walked. You are actually walking thirty to seventy-five feet *above* where Jesus walked. According to one source, Jerusalem has been destroyed and rebuilt at least forty-seven times in the last 3,500 years.

That's the way it is with all earthly cities. Nothing built by man lasts forever. No wonder Abraham was looking for a city built and designed by God. Revelation 21 describes that city as the "new Jerusalem, coming down out of heaven from God" (v. 2). In his vision John saw a city of breathtaking beauty, shining with the glory of God, "its radiance like a most rare jewel, like a jasper, clear as crystal" (v. 11). Christians have always looked to the New Jerusalem as the final abode for the people of God, the place where we will spend eternity together in the presence of the Lord. But note this: Heaven is a *city*. It's a real place filled with real people. That's the city Abraham was looking for when he left Ur of the Chaldees.

Abraham was going to heaven, and he knew it. *That one fact—and that alone—explains his life.*

He had his heart set on heaven, and that explains why he could:

- leave the beautiful city of Ur.
- walk away from his career.
- leave his friends far behind.
- live in tents until the end of his life.
- start all over again in a new land.
- die without seeing all that God had promised.

Abraham knew he was going to heaven, and that changed his whole perspective on life. He knew not just that he was going to die, but that after death he was going to enter a city that God had designed and made.

IS HE CRAZY?

So here's a nice man in his early forties. He has a good job and a great future. He's on the fast track to the top of his field. In a nation where so many live in poverty, he has a nice house, a lovely wife, and six wonderful children. It's a great situation.

One day God says, "I want you to go to America and learn to preach the Word." "Are you talking to me, Lord?" "Yes, I'm talking to you."

When he tells his wife, she says, "Whatever you say, honey." They sell everything and come to America, though people back home beg him to stay. They just shake their heads when he says he is following the call of God.

So what do you think? Is he crazy? Has he lost it? No; he's found it.

He comes because he knows he's going to heaven someday . . . so it doesn't matter so much where he lives in the meantime.

He doesn't plan to die at forty-four. No one ever does. But that's all right too because he knows he's going to heaven when he dies.

"DID WE DO RIGHT?"

The night Lekan died, I went to his house to deliver the sad news. His family and I talked a long time, and his wife, Irene, told me this story: "When he decided to come to America, he told his boss what he was going to do. They didn't want him to leave, so they came to me and said, 'Tell him to stay. Tell him if he stays, we'll make him a General Manager.'"

They came anyway.

That night, looking back, she said, "Did we do right? We came, and he died. Now we're here in America, and he is dead. Did we do right?"

The number two daughter, a seventh-grader, immediately said, "Yes."

"Yes. Better to die as a seminary student than to be General Manager in Nigeria," Irene said.

That, I think, is what the life of faith is all about. It's a decision to live your life in a different way. It's a conscious choice to live for eternity and not for this present life. Please understand: This is *not* idle resignation to martyrdom or suffering. It is a personal choice to follow wherever God leads.

After Lekan died, we discovered a great deal about him we hadn't known before. When he converted from Islam, he dedicated his life to the service of Jesus Christ. And for the ten years before he came to America, he had asked to be transferred to various stations across Nigeria so he could plant churches wherever he worked.

When he came, it was as the hope of his church. He represented the future for the New Salem Church of Nigeria. He would be the anchor for a seminary that would prepare men to preach the Word of God.

DEATH OF A THOUSAND DREAMS

Now he was dead at the age of forty-four, leaving behind a wife and six children. When Lekan died, a thousand dreams died with him. He was the first international student ever to die while enrolled at Dallas Seminary. There was no one from Nigeria to take his place. What would the Nigerians do? How would the church go on? It looked like Satan had won the battle.

A few months later the Nigerians sent two men to visit us in Texas—Pastor Julian and Dr. Jones Fatunwase, the General Superintendent of the New Salem Church. They came halfway around the world just to thank us for what we had done.

At the end of the week, just before I took them to the airport, I said, "Tell me something—is the church in Nigeria stronger or is it weaker now that Lekan has died? You sent him over here, and he died in the middle of his studies. How is the church doing?" The answer came quickly. "Don't you understand? The church is so much stronger now." "How so?" I asked. "When we had the funeral, ten thousand people came from all over Nigeria," Dr. Fatunwase replied. And one of those at the funeral was Lekan's older brother Dele. He was not a Christian. Lekan had prayed for him for ten years. At that funeral, to use my new friend's exact words, Dele Olatoye "decided for Jesus Christ."

In addition, Dr. Fatunwase said, "There were so many people in our churches who had grown complacent." They thought it wasn't that important to live for the Lord. But when they heard how Lekan had died—to use his exact words once again—"a glorious death serving the Lord, hundreds of our people learned it's not how *long* you live, but how *well* you live. Our church in Nigeria is much, much stronger now."

"DIED AT TWENTY-FIVE, BURIED AT SEVENTYFIVE"

How long do you expect to live? To put it more pointedly, how many more years do you think you have left before someone holds your funeral service? Ten years? Twenty years? Thirty years? Forty years? Fifty years? Sixty years? How much of that time are you sure of? The last question is easy. You're not sure about any of it. The truth is, you could die tomorrow—or today—from any of a thousand causes. No one knows how long he or she will live or precisely when he or she will die.

It's not how long you live that matters, but what you do with the years you are given. Too many people die at age twenty-five but aren't buried until they are seventy-five. They waste their best years in trivial pursuits, all the while missing out on the excitement of living by faith.

TWO KINDS OF SUCCESS

Here is the whole chapter in one sentence: *Following God's will doesn't guarantee worldly success.* The operative word is "worldly." God has one view of success; the world has another. Joshua 1:8 reminds us that those who meditate on God's Word will be "prosperous" and successful. Psalm 1 contrasts the fool who looks to the wicked for advice with the godly man who builds his life on the Word of God. The latter will be "like a tree planted by streams of waters." God rewards such a man in this way: "In all that he does, he prospers" (v. 3).

But let's not confuse that with the false notion that doing God's will leads to a trouble-free life. Abraham lived in tents all his life. He died without receiving all that God had promised to him. In many ways you could say that by leaving, he forfeited any chance at worldly greatness. Never again would he know the stability and settled prosperity that he'd had in Ur. From the day he left until the day he died, Abraham was a sojourner, a tent-dweller, a man living on land he did not own.

"THAT'S CRAZY!"

Some time ago a friend called me to talk about a sermon he had heard that tremendously upset him. In the course of the sermon the preacher illustrated his remarks with a story about his decision to go to seminary. He was older than the normal age and had already built a thriving business. After sending in his application, he decided to take a step of faith. He sold his business, moved to a distant city, and invested all his life savings in buying a house. All this without knowing whether or not he would be accepted. At length his faith was rewarded when he was accepted by the seminary. That's the whole story.

To me, it didn't seem very unusual. People do that kind of thing all the time. What surprised me was my friend's reaction to that illustration. To say he was furious would understate the matter. I have never known him to be so upset. "How could anyone do something as stupid as that?" he shouted over the telephone. "That's not faith. That's forcing God's hand." Then he added this comment: "Sure, it worked out for him. But what about all the others who tried it and it didn't work?"

Good question. On one hand, I think my friend was revealing more about himself and his need for earthly security than about the wisdom or folly of what the preacher had done. I've heard similar stories many times, most of them with relatively happy endings. On the other hand, he did raise a good point. There are times when people take a major step of faith only to find that it backfires on them. What if the man hadn't been accepted at seminary? Well, I suppose he would have put his skills to work finding a job in the new city, or perhaps he would have decided to move back where he came from. No shame there. But wouldn't that prove that he was wrong about God's will? Not necessarily. I've already pointed out that nothing worked out for Abraham quite the way he might have expected when he left Ur.

And what about my friend who after a lifetime in Chicago is moving his whole family to another city to start all over again? He and I have already discussed the possibility that things might not work out for him the way he hopes they will. But that's not stopping him from taking the step of faith. I say, bully for him. As much as I might prefer that he stay right where he is, I can hardly stand in the way of a man who truly wants to follow the Lord and is willing to take an unusual step even though things might not work out. No matter what happens, my friend will emerge (I hope and believe) from this experience with a deeper confidence in God because he will be cast upon the Almighty in ways he has not yet known. Either way I think he's going to be all right. But that doesn't preclude some very difficult, scary days of uncertainty as he begins a new life in a new city.

If you ever decide to make God's will the great priority of your life, you will discover that it is indeed an incredible journey. Like Abraham of old, your search for the will of God will lead you out of your comfort zone into the exciting arena of living by faith. Along the way, you will discover that you can indeed survive without absolute certainty about what tomorrow will bring. You may even learn to enjoy living on the edge between faith and absolute disaster. In any case, knowing the will of God will cease to be an academic exercise, like doing your homework before going to bed at night. Instead, it will become the most exciting adventure you've ever known as you set out into the unknown to follow God wherever he leads you.

QUESTIONS FOR PERSONAL/GROUP STUDY

1. Ponder Abraham's dilemma when the Lord called him to leave Ur of the Chaldees. List some reasons why he might have decided not to obey God's call.

2. Do you consider yourself a risk-taker? Why or why not? How do you think you would have responded if you had been in Abraham's shoes?

3. God "called" Abraham to leave Ur. Do you believe he "calls" people in the same way today? What guidelines do you personally follow in order to determine God's call versus your own desires?

4. As you consider the story of Lekan Olatoye, do you know similar stories of others who suffered or died in their attempts to follow God's will? How do you personally react to examples like that? What lessons do you learn?

5. Why is a strong belief in heaven an important part of living by faith and doing God's will?

6. How do you feel about the statement that faith doesn't always mean having 100 percent certainty? Have you ever come to a major decision and taken a step of faith in spite of your doubts? What happened?

GOING DEEPER

Think about your own life for a moment. Where do you need to take decisive action? What holds you back? Write down three areas that need genuine change. Jot down one simple step you could take in each area this week. Then pray this simple prayer: *Lord, I want to follow where you are leading. Grant me courage to step out in faith this week. Amen.*

WHO'S THE BOSS?

The voice on the other end of the phone said, "Pastor Ray, I need to talk to you." It was an old friend from Texas who was visiting his wife's family in Indiana. Could they come by and see us? Yes, of course, we'd be delighted. My friend said he had a big decision to make, and he needed some advice.

I remembered another time four or five years earlier when my friend had come to me with another big decision. Back then he was enrolled in a Master's degree program at a university in the Dallas area. But times were tough; he was out of work and almost out of money. Should he drop out of the program? I asked him one question: "What do you want to do with your life?" When he told me, the answer was easy. Stay in school; do whatever it takes to get your degree; it can only help you get to where you want to go.

In time he got his Master's degree. Still later he became a policeman. He was—and is—a cop. Not just a policeman. My friend is a cop's cop. Tough, no-nonsense, exactly the kind of guy you would want as a partner if you were a policeman and your next call was a drug bust in south Dallas. Eventually he began to pursue the last part of his dream. He entered a Ph.D. program in criminal justice at one of the best universities in America. Taking that step required an enormous sacrifice. He worked five days a week as a policeman, sometimes worked a second job, and often attended classes the final two days of the week. It was not easy, and he didn't see his kids or his wife as much as he—or they—wanted.

"I'M THINKING ABOUT QUITTING"

When he came to see me, he was a third of the way through the program and was finding it far tougher than he'd imagined, even though he had made all A's and one B. He was thinking about quitting because the sacrifice was too great. When I asked if he had a computer to help him write his papers, he said no, he didn't, partly because of the cost and partly because he didn't want to buy a computer if he was going to drop out of the program. As we talked, I sensed he had come to a major crossroads. If he dropped out, he would forever give up the dream. But in order for him to stay in the program, he needed a new vision to make the enormous sacrifice worthwhile.

The turning point came when I asked him how his professors had reacted to his Christian faith. "God has given me favor in their eyes, and every one of them has thanked me for bringing that perspective to my course work," he said. When I heard that, I slammed my hand on the table and exclaimed, "I know exactly what God wants you to do."

ON THE ROAD TO PIGNON

Before I tell you what I said, let me relate another conversation from another time and another place. This one took place in Haiti. It was our final Saturday there, and the team from our church had just visited the Citadelle. It is a national treasure, roughly what you would get if you combined the Washington Monument, the Lincoln Memorial, and the Statue of Liberty. The Citadelle was built by Henri Christophe, the first king of Haiti. It is, as the name implies, a vast fortress sitting astride a mountaintop overlooking the harbor at Cap-Haitien. The king built it in the early 1800s to ward off the French, from whom the people of Haiti had recently won their independence. So remote and treacherous was the location that twenty thousand men died while building it.

We made the trip up the mountain, toured the massive structure, and then hitchhiked down the mountain in the back of a dump truck with the Haitian army band. There were fifty-eight of us—hot, grimy, sweaty, dead-tired, packed like sardines into that dump truck. We hung on for dear life as the driver careened down the side of the mountain, sometimes coming a few inches from a sheer drop-off. The truck let us off at the bottom of the mountain, and we climbed into a smaller pickup truck for the hour and a half trip back to Pignon. Ten kids climbed in the back, and four of us climbed in the front along with Caleb Lucien, our driver.

Somewhere between San Raphael and Pignon, one of the teenagers on our team asked me when I felt called to the ministry. I told her that as a child my hero was Walter Cronkite, the famed CBS newscaster. For many years I dreamed of becoming a journalist. When I became a Christian after my junior year in high school, things began to change. I clearly remember pacing my bedroom floor the month after I graduated from high school wondering what God wanted me to do with my life. One night during that month I woke up in the middle of the night and said, "All right, Lord, if you want me to preach, I'll be a preacher."

That led to a long discussion about how churches today don't hold up God's service as a worthwhile way to spend your life. A generation ago preachers used to call for teenagers to surrender their lives to "full-time Christian service." Almost no one gives that invitation nowadays. We assume our children will choose secular careers; if someone happens to opt for full-time ministry, that's okay, but it's not our first choice. Writer Frederick Buechner tells how, as a young man, he attended a very posh dinner party on Long Island, at which his hostess said to him, "I understand that you are planning to enter the ministry. Is this your own idea, or were you poorly advised?" No doubt many sophisticated people feel the same way.

TOO YOUNG TO GET MARRIED

As we made our way along the bumpy dirt road, I brought up something that a guest speaker had said when he visited our church a few months earlier. It was one of the few truly revolutionary ideas I have heard in the last few years. The speaker said that we ought to encourage our young people to get married earlier. To say that is a stunning piece of advice would be a vast understatement. Before he said that, I had never heard anyone advocate early marriages. Everybody says the opposite—i.e., that early marriages produce early divorces, so kids should wait to get their education first. But the man was dead serious, and whenever a serious person puts forth a revolutionary idea, you have to sit up and think about it.

As I understand it, this was his point: He believes that our modern emphasis on waiting to get married until our children have finished college (and started on their careers) is unbiblical, materialistic, and unrealistic. It is unbiblical because the only reason to remain single is so you can better serve the Lord—not so you can finish college or begin a career (see 1 Corinthians 7). It is materialistic because it puts money ahead of marriage. It is unrealistic because while our kids are waiting to get married, they aren't waiting to have sex.

OUR KIDS AREN'T SAYING NO

On the last point, I think the evidence backs him up 100 percent. Our kids aren't waiting to have sex. Many of them—perhaps most of them—are sexually involved before marriage (and not necessarily with their prospective spouses). Several years ago Josh

McDowell (in cooperation with youth speaker Dawson McAllister) took a nationwide survey of thousands of teenagers from evangelical churches. Here are the results (as summarized by John Nieder in *God, Sex and Your Child* [Nashville: Thomas Nelson, 1988], p. 19):

—By eighteen years of age . . .

43 percent have had sexual intercourse.

39 percent see fondling breasts as morally acceptable.

32 percent see fondling genitals as sometimes morally acceptable.

65 percent have had some kind of sexual contact, from fondling breasts to sexual intercourse.

35 percent could not state that premarital sexual intercourse is always morally unacceptable.

Remember, these are the results from *evangelical* young people. They have been raised in our churches and (presumably) have been taught that premarital sex is always wrong. But somehow the message isn't getting from the head to the heart. The greater point is this: These figures are not significantly different from the figures for the general population.

In one sense, you can hardly blame our kids. After all, we live in a culture that glorifies sex. Apparently it is about to get worse. The Internet has made it possible to view the most degrading images in the privacy of your own home. There are no moral limits. In America anything goes, no matter how vile, how disgusting, how repugnant it may be. While our kids are bombarded with sexual messages encouraging them to "do it," at the same time we are saying to them, "Don't get married too young. Get your education first. Get a career first. *Then* get married." No wonder our kids are confused.

• Our kids aren't getting married.

• But they aren't waiting either.

• Too many of them are "doing it."

We know that the years from fifteen to thirty represent the highest peak of the sexual drive—especially for boys. So at the very point of highest sexual pressure, we say, "Put your education first and make sure you get a career started. Marriage can come later." The result is that our kids put off getting married, and at the same time far too many of them become sexually active.

Why? Is it not in part because we have given them an ungodly reason (get your education first and get your career started) to do a godly thing (abstain from sex before marriage)? Our young people can see right through that charade. They know that behind our pious words stands a very materialistic point of view. When we say that, we have made a false god out of education and career advancement and then beg our kids to "just say no" in order to appease our guilty consciences.

Let us be perfectly clear about the matter. God's answer to uncontrollable sexual desire is marriage (1 Corinthians 7:9). There is nothing wrong or ignoble about that. God's answer to sexual temptation is marriage, *not* waiting until you finally get that B.A. and a good job offer from IBM. When we put education and career above marriage, our kids smell the hypocrisy behind our words. They know that we are really saying, "Put your education and career first, and don't sleep around; but if you do, for heaven's sake, use birth control." After all, we wouldn't want anything like a baby to mess up their career path, would we?

MAKING A CRUCIAL DISTINCTION

Believe it or not, after all this, we're still on the road to Pignon. Caleb now spoke up to disagree strongly with what our guest speaker had said. He argued that early marriages too often lead to broken marriages and that single people can accomplish great things for the Kingdom of God. Those two points are unquestionably true. Were we to shift our view in favor of early marriage, it would require a major rethinking of the church's role in preparation of our young people. But (and this is a big but) that's clearly what happened in Bible times. Scholars tell us that Mary and Joseph were teenagers—probably no older than fourteen or fifteen years old. Early marriages were the norm back then. We have invented a new category called *adolescence* that did not exist until about 130 years ago. In the old days, when you became a teenager you got married.

Caleb himself offers an excellent example of the second point. A native of Haiti, he is a graduate of Washington Bible College and Dallas Theological Seminary (with two degrees). After completing his studies, he went back to Haiti to help his own people. And now he is one of the up-and-coming leaders for the entire country. He is building a Christian camp, has a nationwide radio broadcast, and has plans to found a Christian college to train national leaders. Everywhere we went in Haiti, people stopped to talk to him. He is widely known and greatly loved.

When we had this conversation, he was single but hoped to be married someday. He even had the land picked out for the home he planned to build for his bride-to-be. By his own testimony, he did not have the gift of singleness. A few years later he married Debbie, and they now have two beautiful daughters. And they all live happily in Pignon, Haiti. At the time of our conversation, Caleb believed that he could serve God more effectively as a single person than he could as a married person because he could give all his energies to the work of the Lord. That's basically Paul's argument in 1 Corinthians 7:32-35. I think that today he would say that his marriage and his family are part of his ministry to the world.

How do you bring all of this together? First of all, the guest speaker and Caleb Lucien were talking about two different issues.

• 1. There is such as a thing as marriage in the will of God. Many people should get married to avoid uncontrollable sexual temptation.

• 2. There is also singleness in the will of God. Many people should stay single because they can serve God better that way.

Over the course of a lifetime, people will switch from one category to another. Everyone starts out single, many get married, and some become single again through divorce or the death of their spouse. But it doesn't matter. You can serve God effectively either way. Those who are single do have an advantage in serving the Lord without worldly distractions (that seems to be Paul's point in 1 Corinthians 7), but those who are married can also serve the Lord very effectively.

My point is not to argue in favor of early marriage (although I think we ought to consider this possibility more seriously than we do), but to suggest that having a career in and of itself is not a biblical goal. And when we urge our children to postpone marriage for many years in order to build a career first, we are unwittingly encouraging them in the wrong direction. Serving the Lord through your career is noble. Serving the Lord through marriage is noble. But putting your career above your marriage (or encouraging your children to do that) often leads to bad consequences. Christ must come first in all things.

CROSSING THE LINE

Before going on with the story of my friend from Texas, let's travel back twenty centuries to hear the words of Jesus. The place is Caesarea Philippi, a Roman city located in the Golan Heights, northeast of the Sea of Galilee. A huge rock cliff dominates the landscape. At the base of the cliff a stream flows on its way toward the Jordan River.

It is a critical moment for Jesus. All of Israel is buzzing with word of this man from Galilee. Who is he? By what power does he perform his miracles? What is he really after? After a wave of early popularity, the nation is now divided. True, he has a wide following among the common people. It is also true that among the rich and powerful, opinion is slowly crystallizing against him.

In the distance, the drums of angry opposition are beginning to beat. Before too many months, their sound will become a deafening roar.

Knowing all this, and knowing that it will end in his death, Jesus gathers his disciples in this quiet place to draw out of them a deeper commitment than they have yet given. Jesus looks ahead to the moment he will hang on a Roman cross. What will happen then? Will these men—his inner circle, the men with whom he has spent so much time—stand by him, or will they fall away? Jesus knows the fickleness of the human heart. He also knows that despite their brave words, none of these men can imagine the road they are about to travel together.

It is time to choose sides. These are handpicked men. Jesus has personally trained them. They know him better than anyone else on earth. They have seen him work miracles, watched him heal the sick, marveled as he confounded the Pharisees. But have they grasped the meaning of it all?

It is here—at Caesarea Philippi—that Jesus asks the question, "Who do people say that I am?" (Mark 8:27). And it is here that Peter gives his confession, "You are the Christ, the Son of the living God" (Matthew 16:16).

But the conversation does not end there, for Jesus is seeking more than a *confession*. He is also seeking a *commitment*. "Now that you know who I am, are you willing to commit your life to me?" This is how Jesus puts the issue before the disciples:

And he called to him the crowd with his disciples and said to them, "If anyone would come after me, let him deny himself and take up his cross and follow me. For whoever would save his life will lose it, but whoever loses his life for my sake and the gospel's will save it. For what does it profit a man to gain the whole world and forfeit his life? For what can a man give in return for his life?" (Mark 8:34-37)

WHAT'S THE BEST DEAL?

Take a careful look at those verses in Mark 8. The New International Version rendering for this text uses the word "life" twice, and twice it uses the word "soul." But in the Greek those are not different words. The Greek word is *psyche*, from which we get our English word *psychology*. Sometimes it refers to the immaterial part of man (his soul) as opposed to his body. But more often it refers to the whole man or to the inner, conscious self we call the personality. The *psyche* is the real you that lives and breathes and makes decisions. "Life" (as in the ESV, quoted above) is not a bad translation so long as we remember that it means more than just physical existence.

With that as background, we may paraphrase these verses—and add a bit of twentieth-century idiom—in this way:

> "Now that you know who I am, are you ready to take up your cross and follow me? Before you answer, let me warn you that to follow me will seem in the eyes of the world as if you are wasting your life. The people of the world will never understand what you are doing. It will seem to them that by following me, you are throwing your life away.
>
> "You always have another option. You can try to save your own life by following your own desires. Lots of people do that. They live as if their career is all that matters. But the people who live only for this life will find in the end that they wasted it on things that don't really matter. They tried to save it by living for themselves, but in the end they will lose it. They have wasted their lives on trivial pursuits.
>
> "But if you follow me—though the way will not be easy and you will often be misunderstood—in the end you will save your life. And the people who laugh at you now will not laugh at you then. They will see that you were right and they were wrong.
>
> "After all, what good will it do if you become the richest man in the world or climb to the top of the corporate ladder or

rise to the highest salary level in your company or win the applause of the world—what good will all that do if in the end you find out it was all wasted? What good will that shiny, new sports car do you then? Will you be able to trade it in for another life? No, you won't. But if you want to live that way, go ahead. Millions of people do. In the end they will be sorry, but by then it will be too late to do anything about it.

"So what will it be, men? The way of the cross or the way of the world? You have to invest your life somewhere. What's the best deal you can make?"

THE KNOCK AT THE DOOR

Perhaps a contemporary illustration will help us understand the challenge Jesus gave to his disciples. Not long after the fall of the Soviet Union, I had the privilege of eating supper with a pastor from St. Petersburg, Russia. During the evening he told us what it was like to grow up in a Communist country. His father (a pastor for over forty years) used to tell his mother, "Some night we may be sleeping when suddenly there will come a knock at the door. When that happens, don't be surprised if the KGB takes me away in the middle of the night and you never see me again. When that happens, don't give up the faith. After I am gone, remember that the Lord will never leave you."

During the Communist years many Christians were taken to the prison camps and psychiatric hospitals and were made to suffer horribly simply because of their faith. Some believers spent twenty-five years or more behind bars for the sake of the Gospel. A few of them came out and wrote books about their experiences. But most of those who suffered for God did not write any books because they did not want any publicity. They viewed their time in prison as part of their ministry for God. Their attitude was, "If God can use me more effectively in the Gulag, then that's where I will serve him."

After seventy years of oppression, the people of Russia are still getting used to freedom. Many western Christians are bothered by one question: Why would God allow the Communists to oppress the people for seventy years? There are many negative answers to that question; but around the dinner table that night, the pastor offered a positive answer that went something like this:

> "After all that has happened to us, the church in Russia is almost like the first-century apostolic church. We have nothing but a pure faith in God. Our churches are not corrupted by many things that corrupt churches in the West. I believe that a great revival is coming to the world in the last days, and I believe that the Russian church will send out thousands of missionaries around the world. In order for us to be ready for that, we had to be oppressed by the Communists."

That is part of what it means to "lose [your] life" for Jesus' sake. Though it may cost you dearly in terms of this world's goods, in the end you will accomplish far more than if you had taken the easy road.

Was Jesus a Failure?

What is the best deal you can make? The life of Jesus is the best answer to that question. Consider the facts of His "career":

• He was born in an obscure village in an out-of-the-way province of the Roman Empire.

• He never went to college, nor did he have any professional training.

• He never had a bank account.

• He owned no property except the clothes on his back.

• He never held public office.

• He never wrote a book.

• He never had a wife or children.

• His closest friends were blue-collar workers.

• He felt at home among the outcasts of society.

• His ministry consisted of preaching in the countryside, teaching in the synagogues, answering difficult questions, healing the sick, and casting out demons.

• His opponents openly accused him of consorting with the devil.

• Along the way, he made many powerful enemies by exposing corruption in high places.

• Finally, his adversaries captured him, tried him in a kangaroo court, and put him to death.

To be perfectly honest, by most modern standards we would consider him a failure. He never made it to the top. If ever a man seemed to waste his life, it was Jesus.

But consider this. After more than two thousand years . . .

• His words are remembered and repeated around the world.

• His followers number in the hundreds of millions and can be found in every country on earth.

• His personal integrity stands unsullied amidst the attacks of the cynics and the sneers of the ignorant.

• His death, which seemed to be a tragedy, has become the means by which we can be reconciled to God.

• His whole mission on earth, which seemed to be a failure, has now become history's greatest success story.

How can this be? He was humiliated to the point of death and seemed to lose his life for no purpose whatsoever. And yet through his death God exalted him to the very highest position in the universe, "so that at the name of Jesus every knee should bow, in heaven and on earth and under the earth, and every tongue confess that Jesus Christ is Lord, to the glory of God the Father" (Philippians 2:10-11).

Jesus made clear why he did what he did when he said, "Unless a grain of wheat falls into the earth and dies, it remains alone; but if it dies, it bears much fruit" (John 12:24). Out of one seed comes forth a vast harvest; but that seed must die in order to bring forth fruit. As long as the seed "saves" its life, it remains alone. But when it "loses" its life, it brings forth the harvest.

It's simple, really. If you try to "save" your life, in the end you "lose" it. But if you dare to "lose" it for Jesus' sake, in the end you "save" it. Jesus himself is the supreme example of this principle.

CAREER VS. MISSION

There is yet another way of looking at this whole question of losing and saving your life. Let me do it by asking this question: *Is your life a career or a mission?*

There is a vast difference between those two concepts. A quick glance at a dictionary reveals the essence of the difference:

• A career is something *you choose* for yourself.
• A mission is something *chosen for you* by someone else.

For the sake of convenience, we can display many of the differences this way:

CAREER	MISSION
Chosen by you	Chosen by God
Do something	Be something
Your goals for your life	God's goals for your life
"I can do it"	"Bigger than me"
"I want it all right now"	"I'm willing to wait for God"
Ladder to climb	Journey to take
Present satisfaction	Future fulfillment
Horizontal focus	Vertical focus
Tangible rewards	Intangible rewards
Happiness	Joy
Destination primary	Journey primary
"My career is my life"	"My mission is my life"
"I am a professional"	"I am a disciple"
Make a mark	Do God's will
Make it to the top	Take up the cross
"My kingdom come"	"Thy kingdom come"

Build a fortune	Lay up treasures in heaven
Focus: performance	Focus: relationship with God
Market-driven	Holiness-driven
Image-conscious	God-conscious

There is a huge difference between living for your career and being sent on a mission. The Bible never talks about having a career. Having a career is *not* a biblical issue. Having a mission is.

IS THAT ALL THERE IS?

It is not that believers don't have careers. We do. Some of us are painters, some are doctors, some are computer scientists, some are bankers, some are nurses, some are teachers, and some are writers. Some are homemakers and mothers (an honorable and often-overlooked career). But the difference is this: *The people of the world live for their careers; the people of God don't.*

When your career is the most important factor in your life, then you are career-driven and career-minded while you climb the career ladder. You take a job and leave it two years later because it's "a good career move." You break all the significant relationships in one place and move across the country because your career demands it. Everything is calculated to get you someday to that elusive place called "The Top." When you get there, your career will be complete, and the world will applaud your achievements.

I am suggesting that being career-minded in this sense is precisely what Jesus meant when he said, "Whoever would save his life will lose it." Your career may well keep you from fulfilling your mission in life; and your mission may never make much sense as a career.

• Your career is the answer to the question, "What do I do for a living?"

• Your mission is the answer to the question, "What am I doing with my life?"

If you are just here to eat, sleep, go to college, get a degree, get married, get a job, have some children, climb the corporate ladder, make some money, buy a summer home, retire gracefully, grow old, and die . . . then what's the big deal? All of that is okay; but if that's all there is to life, you are really no different from pagans who don't even believe in God.

Let's put it this way: Jesus calls his followers to be totally sold out to his Kingdom. That applies to *all* Christians *all* the time, not just to "full-time Christian workers" such as pastors or missionaries. Suppose you are an electrical engineer or an attorney. Here is God's job description for you:

• You are a missionary cleverly disguised as an engineer.
• You are a missionary cleverly disguised as an attorney.

It's nice to have a career; it's far better to be on a mission for God.

It's not wrong to have a career and do well by the world's standards. Nor is it sinful to move across the country. I've already shared the story of my good friend who is moving away from Chicago because he is truly attempting to follow God's will for his life. But motivation is everything. Two people may follow the same career path, and both may end up at the top. Yet one may be living solely for his career, while the other sees his life as a divinely ordained mission from God. One has lost his life; the other has saved it, just as Jesus said.

Ask yourself, did Jesus have a career? No; he had a mission from God to be the Savior of the world. Nothing he did makes sense from a career point of view. Being crucified is not a good career move. Yet by his death he reconciled the world to God. Was he a success or a failure? The answer is obvious.

A MAN WITH A MISSION

So I slapped my hand on the table and said to my friend, "I know exactly what God wants you to do. He wants you to go back to

Texas, get back into that Ph.D. program, get your degree, and go make a difference in the criminal justice system of America. Do you understand the position you're in? We all agree that the criminal justice system is corrupt in America, and we all agree it needs reforming. But how? And who will do it? I can't do it. I'm just a layman when it comes to criminal justice. I can say all I want, but the professionals won't listen to me. I don't know anything about the ins and outs of criminal justice. Everything I know I get by watching *Perry Mason* reruns. I have no influence whatsoever.

"We need men and women who believe the Bible, who are trained at the very highest level in criminal justice, who are willing to pay the price in time and sacrifice to get the degree from the best schools in America, who unashamedly bring their evangelical faith into the classroom and attempt—however imperfectly—to proclaim the lordship of Jesus Christ over our criminal justice system. Where can we find such men and women? They would have to be born-again Christians. They would have to be trained in the Bible. They would have to be unafraid to speak out. They would have to go through the most rigorous training. They would have to pay the price up front in order to make an impact later.

"We truly need men and women like that in order to make an impact on the criminal justice system in America. Where will we find them? You fit all those criteria. And you are about to quit the program. Don't quit. You can make a difference for the Kingdom of God within the criminal justice system. We can always get more Christian cops, but where will we get enough highly-trained people ready to speak out for God to the criminal justice system? Stay in school and get your degree."

He looked startled, and then a grin slowly spread across his face. "Pastor, I never thought about it like that. I guess I was just thinking about getting my degree and going to teach somewhere. I never thought about it as a mission from God."

Then I said, "If you are just going to get your degree so you can teach somewhere, forget it—we have enough professors already. If getting your Ph.D. is just a career move, forget it—it's not worth the sacrifice. But if you believe God has called you to make a difference for him within the criminal justice system, then you need that Ph.D. in order to speak to the system with total credibility. It all depends on whether you want a career or a mission."

A BRAND-NEW COMPUTER

My friend returned to Texas, and I wondered what he would do. About a month later he wrote me a letter saying that he had decided to go ahead and complete the program. And he added an interesting footnote.

Once he decided to finish the program, he knew he needed to go ahead and buy a computer. So he shopped around and found what he thought was a good deal. One Sunday while attending church he happened to mention his plans to buy a computer. A man hearing his story said, "Give me the details, and I'll have one of my people check it out for you." My friend gave the man the details about the system he proposed to buy, and the man gave it to one of his employees.

A few days later the man came back and said, "This isn't the best deal. Here is what you really need . . ." The hardware and the software the man proposed cost several hundred dollars more than the system my friend already couldn't afford.

Before my friend could say anything, the man said, "My wife and I have decided we would like to buy this computer system for you as our investment in your life." That's what happens when you stop looking at your life as a career and start viewing it as a mission. People catch the vision and rally to your support.

THE GREATEST MISSION ON EARTH

As we wrap up this chapter, let me suggest several implications of the truth about losing your life for Christ. First, *we need to challenge our teenagers to see themselves as being on a mission for God.* Too many times we talk as if having a career is what life is all about. But why bother staying pure if your ultimate purpose in life is to get an education so you can start a career and build a fortune? Where is the motive for saying no to temptation? Our only hope is to challenge the next generation to lose their lives for Jesus' sake. Then and only then will they have the spiritual resources to stand up against the incoming tidal wave of evil. Why lose your life in pursuit of an MBA just so you can retire to Florida in forty-five years? Big deal. Life ought to add up to something more than that.

Let's start challenging our children to a standard far higher than the empty call of materialism. Let's tell them about the only thing that really matters in life—following Jesus in the greatest mission on earth.

Second, *every Christian needs to do a career/mission inventory from time to time.* Too often we agonize over God's will because we have a career orientation instead of a mission orientation. So we make our decisions strictly from a worldly basis regarding money, position, influence, titles, salary, benefits, staying on the right career path, backing the right people, and so on. But Jesus has already warned us that you can have all those things and still lose your own soul. Following Christ is the way to life!

The question is not, what are you doing for a living? The deeper issue is, what are you doing with your life? Why did God put you here on the earth?

A quick illustration may help. A friend took me out to lunch recently to share what God is doing in his life. My friend served for about ten years as an international business consultant. Along the way he worked with several multinational corporations in England, Brazil, and Italy. Right now he is in transition, beginning his own consulting firm in the Midwest. In talking about what it means to be a Christian in the business world, my friend made a comment that stuck in my mind: "If you are happy and productive in your current job, the only reason to take a promotion is to leverage your position for the Kingdom of God."

That's a tremendous insight. Use the bigger position to impact the world for Jesus Christ. Don't just climb the ladder in order to get to the top. Realize that God has put you where you are "for such a time as this" (Esther 4:14). Understand that behind every open door and every promotion stands the Lord God who rules heaven and earth. As you climb to the top, remember who put you there.

Too many Christians routinely make wrong decisions because they are too career-minded and not mission-focused. What a huge difference it makes to see all of life as belonging to the Lord Jesus Christ!

THE ANSWER MAKES ALL THE DIFFERENCE

The martyred missionary Jim Elliot said, "He is no fool who gives what he cannot keep to gain what he cannot lose." If you try to save your life, you'll lose it in the end. If you lose your life for Jesus' sake, in the end you will save it.

If you live for your career, what difference will it make ten seconds after you die? If you spend your life in the service of the Kingdom of God, the road may not be easy, but ten thousand years from now you won't regret your decision.

Do you have a career, or are you on a mission for God? The answer to that question makes all the difference in the world.

QUESTIONS FOR PERSONAL/GROUP STUDY

1. Most people agree that getting a good education is absolutely vital. But how much education is enough? In the major story of this chapter, the man eventually got his Ph.D. Few of us will go that far. What biblical principles should guide our decisions regarding how much education we need?

2. When should career issues enter into the picture? How do we factor in the "mission for God" principle?

3. Across the centuries some skeptics have mocked Jesus as a misguided rabbi whose life was a dismal failure. What evidence could you muster to support such a charge? How would you refute it? In your opinion, what was the mission of Jesus Christ? Did he succeed or fail? Explain your answer.

4. How do you evaluate the author's discussion of early marriage vs. building a career first?

5. Since all of us will have a career of one kind or another, how can we ensure that our career is part of our mission in life? Could two people have the same career and perhaps even work side-by-side, and yet one is on a mission for God and the other is simply climbing the career ladder? How would the difference between the two be seen in daily life?

6. Read Mark 8:34-38 carefully. Now imagine that Jesus is speaking to you personally. Paraphrase his words as you imagine he would say them if the two of you were talking together. How do these words apply to your interests, hobbies, career aspirations, and relationships?

GOING DEEPER

Have you discovered your mission in life? Not your career, but the basic reason God put you on this earth. How does your life stack up against the career vs. mission comparison in this chapter? Set aside ten minutes a day for the next week to think and pray about God's mission for your life. Factor in your natural talents, your spiritual gifts, the major events (both good and bad) of your life, and your answer to the question, "What is God's purpose for my life?" Then write a one-sentence mission statement. Write it down, and place the statement where you can see it every day. Memorize it, and share it with at least one other person. You may be surprised to see your life taking on a new, more purposeful direction.

THE HARDEST PRAYER
YOU WILL EVER PRAY

Some prayers are harder to pray than others. I learned that thirty years ago when my father died. One October day he felt a pain in his shoulder. The doctors later said it was transferred pain from a bacterial infection elsewhere in his body. It did not seem serious at first, but he got no better and a few days later traveled by ambulance to Birmingham, where a battery of doctors went to work on him. Marlene and I drove in from Dallas, arriving at the hospital sometime after midnight. Dad spoke to me when I saw him, but I could tell he was desperately ill.

A few days later, now back in Dallas, we received the dreaded call. Once again we sped through the night to Birmingham, hoping against hope. But my untrained eyes told me that he was not long for this world. That day—it is etched forever in my mind—I went in to see him, and he did not know me. He was drugged and nearly in a coma. Leaning against the wall outside the Intensive Care Unit I wept furious tears, unable to keep back the truth—my dad was dying, and I could do nothing about it.

I must have prayed that day. I'm sure I did. After all, I was in seminary learning to help other people draw near to God. But I didn't pray with words. In that terrible moment of utter helplessness, prayer did not come naturally. All theology aside, I knew my father was dying. I could hardly pray, "O God, heal him," for I knew in my soul that God was not going to answer that prayer. I could not pray, "O God, take him home and end the pain," for he was my father and much too young to die. I prayed, "O God," but that's about all. In a few days God mercifully intervened and ended my father's ordeal.

PRAYING IN THE DARKNESS

Most people have been in the same place. Perhaps you have. You have stood beside the bed of a loved one and found that prayer was nearly impossible. Or you have faced a difficulty so immense that you truly did not know what words to use when you prayed. Or perhaps there have been times in your life when you have not prayed because you were afraid of the answer God would give.

Prayer can do that to even the best of us. It seems easy on Sunday morning. Why is it so difficult to pray in the darkness? Perhaps we are afraid of what God will say in response to our prayers. What if we ask for guidance and he guides us in ways we don't want to follow? What if we pray for wisdom and the wisdom we receive seems more like nonsense? What if we pray for patience and the answer means nothing but trouble for us?

A LITTLE MORE LIKE THE ANGELS

All of this should not surprise us. Jesus hinted at the problem when he gave us the Lord's Prayer. Included in that model prayer were these words: "Your kingdom come, your will be done, on earth as it is in heaven" (Matthew 6:10). The basic difficulty may be easily seen if we lay it out in a series of logical statements:

1. God has a will concerning my life.
2. God's will encompasses his desires for my life.
3. But I also have a will that encompasses my desires for my life.

4. Those two wills are often in conflict with each other.

5. When there is a conflict, either God's will or my will will prevail.

6. When I pray, "Your will be done," I am asking for God's will to prevail over my will.

That's the basic difficulty we face when we pray. *When we ask that God's will be done, we are implicitly asking that our wills be overturned, if necessary.* It's not easy to pray that way when you're standing beside the hospital bed of someone you love.

But that's only part of the problem. Jesus taught us to pray that God's will might be done "on earth as it is in heaven." Exactly how is God's will being done in heaven? If the reference is to the angels (as I think it is), then God's will is *always* being done in heaven. Psalm 103:20 says, "Bless the LORD, O you his angels, you mighty ones who do his word, obeying the voice of his word!" In heaven, God's will is *always* done; in heaven, God's will is *instantaneously* done; in heaven, God's will is *completely* done; in heaven, God's will is *joyfully* done. In essence, Jesus asks us to pray that we might become a little more like the angels (who always obey) and a little less like the demons (who never obey). When that happens, the earth will become a little more like heaven and a little less like hell.

But God's will is rarely done on the earth. After all, there are over five billion wills on the earth and still only one will in heaven. Just look around you. Do you see God's will being done? Pick up the newspaper and read about a serial killer. Read about the killing in Iraq, the slaughter in Sudan, the corruption in high places in America, the rise of satanic ritual child abuse. It looks like someone else's will is being done.

In some ways, "Your will be done" seems like the most hopeless of all prayer requests. Seldom do we mean it. Seldom does it seem to be answered.

"Your will be done" is a difficult prayer to pray sincerely. It may be the hardest prayer you will ever pray. Even though Jesus himself instructed us to use these words, there are at least four reasons why we find it difficult to do so.

Reason #1:
It is hard to pray, "Your will be done" because it means giving up control of your own life

We're back to that little syllogism again:

1. God has a will (or desire) for your life.
2. But you also have a will (or desire) for your life.
3. When you pray, "Your will be done," you are asking that his will take precedence over yours.

Only one will can be done at a time. Either God calls the shots or you call the shots. Either he is in control or you are in control. It's not easy to pray like that because it means giving up control of your own life.

But you aren't really in control anyway. It only seems that way.

PROVERBS 20:24

Recently I helped officiate in a wedding ceremony for two students attending a local Christian college. During the rehearsal I had a nice talk with a professor from that college, who was also taking part in the ceremony. In the course of our conversation he brought up a verse I had never considered before—Proverbs 20:24 ("A man's steps are from the LORD; how then can man understand his way?"). That didn't seem remarkable until the professor mentioned that the word for "man" in the first part of the verse is not the usual Hebrew word. It is a Hebrew word that means "a mighty warrior." The Old Testament writers used that particular word to speak of great soldiers who marched valiantly into battle. These were the "mighty men" of Israel who possessed great strength and courage.

We could legitimately translate the first part of the verse this way: "Even the steps of a mighty man are directed by the Lord." Think of the "mighty men" of this decade. Their names are George W. Bush, Colin Powell, Tony Blair, Vladimir Putin, and, in another category, Bill Gates, Brad Pitt, Derek Jeter, Peyton Manning, and Donald Trump. As I'm writing these words, those names are currently among the "mighty men" of the world. But in a few years (maybe just one or two), the list will change. In twenty years the list may be entirely different. They all appear to be self-made men, self-sufficient, able to run their own lives. But it only appears that way. Solomon says that behind the power and image of the mighty man stands the Lord himself. He is the one who directs their paths.

That brings us to the second half of the verse: "How then can anyone understand his own way?" (NIV). The word translated "anyone" (ESV, "man") is actually the normal Hebrew word for "man." In this context, it has the idea of "mere mortal man." If even the mighty man cannot direct his own steps, how then can any of us be sure about the future? If the people we look up to are at the mercy of higher hands, then how can any of us claim to fully understand the direction of our lives? The answer is, we can't. The mighty man can't. The average man can't. You can't. I can't. No one can.

DAVE DRAVECKY

Consider Dave Dravecky. In the late 1980s he was one of the rising stars of professional baseball. He pitched for the San Diego Padres and later for the San Francisco Giants. His future seemed bright as he won game after game with a blazing fastball and a mean curve that dipped and dropped as it passed over home plate.

Then it happened. A strange soreness in his left arm. An examination. A biopsy. Cancer. Just like that, his career seemed in jeopardy. Surgery was followed by months of rehabilitation.

Then a stint in the minor leagues. Then his great comeback game. Five days later he pitched in Montreal. No one who has seen the video will ever forget it. He threw a pitch, and his weakened bone snapped. This time there would be no coming back.

Several months later the doctors removed his left arm and a large part of his left shoulder. It was the only way to rid his body of cancer once and for all. After the surgery he issued a brief statement thanking his many friends and fans for their love and prayers. He said he looked forward to a life free from pain.

A "TEMPORARY SETBACK"

There was no further word until he spoke at a convention in Orlando. His words were reported by newspapers and TV stations around the country. To Dave Dravecky, his amputation was just a "temporary setback." He said he planned to swim and play golf and tennis now that he is no longer playing baseball. He also planned to continue speaking around the country.

At a time when many people would be drowning in self-pity, Dave Dravecky was looking to the future. "There is no struggle about feeling sorry for myself. The question is not, 'Why me, God?' The question is, 'What is Your plan for me?'" Then he answered his own question: "I see this as God giving me the opportunity to share the Gospel with a lot of people."

Many positive lessons can be drawn from his example. For our purposes I will point out just one: No one, not even a mighty man like Dave Dravecky, directs his own path. Surely he would not have chosen the path the Lord chose for him. Who would choose to have cancer and lose an arm? But Dave Dravecky's path was directed by the Lord. It is entirely to his credit that he understands that fact and publicly glorifies God in a circumstance that would have embittered many other people.

"Every Day I Pray, 'Thy Will Be Done'"

I'm thinking of another man right now—not as well-known as Dave Dravecky—but a "mighty man" in his own right. For many years he has been rising to the top of his profession. I do not know his salary, but I am sure he is well-compensated for his labors. Recently we ate lunch together. His outward prosperity is only part of the story. In his life he has known more than his share of pain and sorrow. Tragedy struck close to home once and then twice. He is outgoing and friendly, and you feel drawn to him immediately; but if you look closely at his eyes, there is heaviness there. He bears burdens about which only his close friends know.

Right now he's in the middle of great turmoil in the place where he works. The details don't matter. But every day he faces the reality of going to work knowing that his superiors have not appreciated his contributions to the firm. It's a real battle to get up, go to work, and keep a smile on his face.

But he looked so relaxed when I ate lunch with him. How does he do it? A great change has come across his life in the last few days. It's a change on the inside, a change in the way he looks at things. "Pastor, I've been pushing and pushing and pushing. Trying to fix things up. Trying to make a better deal. Holding all my cards, dealing them out one by one. It hasn't worked. The Lord finally said to me, 'Why don't you let me take over?' So I did. I told the Lord he could take over. Nothing has changed at the office. Things are going to get worse before they get better. They're going to make things miserable for me. But that doesn't matter. I've given it all to the Lord. That means I don't have to figure out all the details of my future." Then he said, "I'm going to relax now." He's a good man in a hard place. But you wouldn't know it to look at him. Somehow he has grasped the great truth that praying, "Your will be done" means letting go of your own life. My friend has learned it the same way we all have to learn it—through hard experience.

As we were walking back to his car, he said, "Every day I pray this simple prayer, 'Thy will be done.'" No wonder he has a smile on his face. It's hard to pray that prayer because it means giving up control of your life. But that doesn't mean your life will go out of control. It just means that your life is surrendered to God's control.

Reason #2:
It is hard to pray, "Your will be done" because we often doubt that God wants the best for us

There is a second reason why this is a difficult prayer to pray. If the first one touches our will, the second one touches our mind. The first reason was practical; the second is theological. Oftentimes we're scared that if we give God control of our lives, he'll mess it up somehow. We wouldn't say it that way, but that's how we really feel.

More than once I have heard people say, "Pray for the opposite of what you want, because God always gives us the opposite of what we ask for." We laugh when we read that because it seems so absurd. But many of us secretly wonder if it isn't true. We've all known the frustration of unanswered prayer. Perhaps it was for something small—like a new dress for a Saturday night date. Perhaps it was for God to give you a basset hound. Perhaps you asked God to open the door for you to go to a certain college. Or perhaps it was for something truly big—prayer requested at the bedside of a loved one, prayer for a wayward child, prayer for a failing marriage. When God doesn't answer our prayers— or when he doesn't answer in the way we want him to—are we not tempted to wonder if God gives us the opposite of what we ask for?

DOES GOD KNOW MY NAME?

Our biggest problem is not, is there a God? Virtually everyone agrees that the answer is yes. Even people who never come to church and people who consider themselves irreligious would answer yes. Here is the bigger question: Is there a God in heaven who cares about me? Millions of people—including millions of apparently loyal churchgoers—secretly wonder if the answer to that question might be no. A God who is there—yes. A God who cares for me—maybe not.

Perhaps some wonder if this does not reveal a kind of spiritual schizophrenia. How can you answer yes to one question and no or maybe not to the other? Is this not some kind of internal contradiction? If there is a God, surely he cares about me. And if he doesn't care for me, who cares whether there's a God or not?

But those questions reside on two different levels. The existence of God is primarily a mental or logical problem. It's an issue of philosophy. The question concerning God's personal concern is entirely different. Very often it is asked by those who have known deep pain and suffering. For them the question is very personal: "If God cares for me, how could he let my son die?" Or, "where was God when my husband lost his job?" Or, "why didn't God keep that man from shooting my father?" These are not abstract questions about first causes and the argument from design. These are questions wrenched from the depths of horrible despair.

How do you pray, "Your will be done" when you aren't sure that God really cares about you? If you knew—really knew—that he had your best interests at heart, you might dare to pray that way. But as long as you doubt, that prayer will be almost impossible.

HE BOWED HIS HEAD AND DIED

There are many answers to the question, does God really care for me? But there is only one that really matters. It's the answer God gave two thousand years ago on a hill outside the city walls of Jerusalem. On a hot Friday afternoon the Romans crucified a man they thought to be a Jewish rabble-rouser. Only later did they understand who he really was. His name was Jesus. He came from a small town in Galilee called Nazareth. He started his ministry by preaching in the synagogues. As he went from village to village, his fame spread, until thousands came out to hear him. At length the powers-that-be found him to be a threat to them, and they decided to eliminate him. It took a long time to trap him, but they finally arrested him with the help of a traitor from his inner circle.

Once arrested, he was tried, beaten, mocked, insulted, cursed, abused, slapped, scourged, and crowned with thorns. Eventually he was condemned to die. For six hours he hung on a cross—naked before the world, exposed to the elements, reviled by the crowd, jeered by his enemies, mourned by those who loved him. At the end, after suffering excruciating pain, he bowed his head and died.

HIS NAME IS FATHER

After all that, God says, "Do you still wonder if I love you?"

For some people, even the death of God's Son will not be enough. But if that is not enough, nothing God can do will make any difference. For if someone will give his own Son to die, is there anything else he will hold back? Money is nothing compared to a son.

That's why the most crucial word of the Lord's Prayer is in the very first phrase—"Our *Father* in heaven." To call God *Father* means that you recognize what he did when he gave his own Son to die on the cross. *Father* is not some word to toss around when we pray. It's what Christian prayer is all about. God is worthy to be called "Father" precisely because he has done what good fathers must do—he has sacrificed the best that he had for the welfare of his children.

Look to the cross, my doubting friend. Gaze on the Son of God. Ponder the meaning of Golgotha. Who is the one crucified on Calvary's tree? His name is Jesus. Study his face. See the wounds in his hands, his feet, his side. Was it not for you that he died? Do you still doubt that God loves you?

That's the second reason why this prayer is difficult. Many of us doubt that God truly cares for us. The third reason moves us into a completely different arena.

Reason #3:
It is hard to pray, "Your will be done" because God's will sometimes involves suffering and pain

That was true for Jesus. The scene has shifted from Jesus' giving his disciples a model prayer to Thursday night. It is late—perhaps 10:30 or 11:00 P.M. The Lord now retreats to his favorite spot—the olive groves in Gethsemane. Leaving Peter, James, and John behind, he wrestles in prayer with what is about to happen. He knows with the perfect knowledge of omniscience that the time has come for him to die. All is revealed; nothing is hidden. It was for this moment that he came into the world. Nothing will surprise him—not Judas' wicked kiss, not Caiaphas' mocking words, not Pilate's curious questions. The pain, the blood, the anguish—all of it is as clear to him as if it had already happened.

Most of all he sees the darkness. Sin like a menacing cloud hovers over him. *Sin!* The very word is repugnant to him. Sin in all its ugliness, all its vile reaches, all its putrefying force, now looms before him. It is as if a giant sewer is being opened, and the foul contents are flooding over him. All the evil that men can do, all the filth of uncounted atrocities, the swill of the human race, the total iniquity of every man and woman from the beginning of time!

As Jesus sees the cup filled with human scum approaching him, he recoils in horror. These are his words: "My Father, if it be possible, let this cup pass from me; nevertheless, not as I will, but as you will" (Matthew 26:39). These are not the words of unbelief. They are words of faith. They are the words of a man who understands fully what it will cost to do the will of God.

Was it wrong for Jesus to pray this way? Did it somehow reveal a lack of trust in God? I think not. No one has ever been more committed to doing the will of God. He did not pray because he wished to be released from the will of God. He prayed because he knew how much the will of God would cost him personally. He was willing to pay the price, but in the horror of seeing the "cup" of suffering draw near, he asked that it might be removed from him.

If Jesus in his extremity struggled with the will of God, should we be surprised if we do the same? If it was difficult for Jesus to pray, "Your will be done," is it likely to be any easier for us? Jesus is Exhibit A of what it costs to pray, "Your will be done." It cost him his life. No wonder he struggled in Gethsemane.

THE UNDERGROUND CHURCH

Several years ago *Reader's Digest* carried a lead article entitled "China's Daring Underground of Faith" (August 1991, pp. 33-38). It told the story of Pastor Lin Xiangao, one of the leaders of the underground church movement in China. When the Communists took over in 1949, most Christian workers fled the country. Pastor Lin was offered a safe parish in Hong Kong but turned it down, preferring to stay in Canton with his own people. Already there were rumors of mass executions, but Pastor Lin stayed because "I felt it was my duty to suffer for the Lord."

The knock on his door came in 1955. He was jailed for sixteen months, released, jailed again, and held in various labor camps until 1978. Soon after getting out, he resumed his ministry, building a congregation of hundreds of people. Now we will fast-forward to 1990.

Following an evening service on February 22, 1990, policemen burst into Lin's tiny house. They confiscated all the Bibles and hand-stenciled tracts, along with hymnals, tapes and recorders, an organ, and a mimeograph machine. They also seized his membership lists.

Government officials warned Lin's followers not to attend his services, and he was ordered to stop preaching. For a time he complied. But he struggled inwardly and finally felt called to preach again. As he resumed his ministry, the police summoned him for numerous interrogations. To all demands Lin replied quietly, "I have spent twenty years in your prisons. I fear nothing anymore."

The writer of the article ends his story this way:

> As I left Lin Xiangao's home, I asked him if he thought he would be jailed again. "Perhaps," he replied. "But we are Christians and difficulty brings us closer to Christ." He paused for a moment and then added simply, "Pray for us." (p. 38)

Don't let that last phrase slip by you. "We are Christians and difficulty brings us closer to Christ." Here is a brother who understands what it means to pray, "Your will be done." He knows how hard it is, but he has prayed the prayer anyway.

"Your will be done" *is* a hard prayer to pray. Jesus knew it. Pastor Lin knows it. Blessed are those who know it and pray the prayer anyway.

Reason #4:
It is hard to pray, "Your will be done"
because you are praying against the status quo

God's will is seldom done on the earth. Too many things that go on are obviously not God's will. Abortion . . . crack babies . . . broken homes . . . rampant pornography . . . men starving, women freezing, children wearing rags . . . racial prejudice . . . ethnic hatred . . . serial killers on the loose . . . corruption in high places.

Sometimes it seems as if God has gone to sleep and Satan has taken over. Now ponder the next sentence carefully: *God does not accept the status quo.* He does not accept Satan's usurpation of God's rightful place in the world. He does not accept that sin should reign forever on the earth. He does not accept that the killing should go on forever. God does not sit idly by while the world goes to hell.

God does not accept the status quo!

In fact, he sent his own Son into the world to change the status quo. What the prophets couldn't accomplish with their words, his Son accomplished by the Incarnation. At Bethlehem God sent a message to the world: "Things are going to change."

If things were okay, why did God send his Son? But things weren't okay. They were wrong, dreadfully wrong, and getting worse all the time. So God intervened in human history in the most dramatic fashion possible.

NO SAINTLY RESIGNATION

To pray, "Your will be done" is to follow God in opposing the status quo. This prayer goes against the grain. In a world where God's will is *not* done, we are to pray that the will of God *will* be done. Those are fighting words, words that rebel against everything that is evil and wrong on Planet Earth. All too often when we pray, "Your will be done," we do it with an air of pious resignation: "O God, since I am helpless to stem the tide of events, may your will be done." Sometimes we use it as an excuse not to get angry at the sin and suffering all around us.

But if God does not accept the status quo, neither should we!

Let me say it plainly: To pray, "Your will be done" is an act of God-ordained rebellion! This is not a prayer for the weak or the timid. This is a prayer for troublemakers and rabble-rousers. It is a prayer for believers who look at the devastation all around them and say, "I'm angry, and I'm not going to take this lying down."

It is a prayer, then, that leads necessarily to action. If you see injustice being done, you cannot blithely pray, "Your will be done" and then walk away. If you really mean, "Your will be done," you have to jump into the fray and help make it happen.

YOU'LL NEVER KNOW UNTIL YOU LET GO

Let me summarize everything I've said in this chapter: "Your will be done" is hard to pray. There are at least four reasons:

1. It is hard because it means you have to give up control of your own life.
2. It is hard because many of us doubt that God truly cares for us.
3. It is hard because God's will may involve pain and suffering.
4. It is hard because God's will is so often not done in this world.

Every point is true. And yet Jesus told us to pray this way.

It's not wrong to struggle with this prayer. After all, Jesus struggled with it himself. But over the years I've discovered that the happiest people are those who have said, "I've decided to let go and let God run my life." So many of us go through life with a clenched fist, trying to control the uncontrollable, trying to mastermind all the circumstances, trying to make our plans work. So we hold tightly to the things we value—our career, our reputation, our happiness, our health, our children, our education, our wealth, our possessions, even our mates. We even hold tightly to life itself. But those things we hold so tightly never really belonged to us in the first place. They always belonged to God. He loaned them to us, and when the time comes he will take them back again.

Happy are those people who hold lightly the things they value greatly. The happiest people I know are those who have said, "All right, Lord, I'm letting go. I'm going to relax now and let you take over."

What are you struggling with right now? What are you holding on to so tightly that it almost makes your hands hurt? What is it that you are afraid to give to God? Whatever it is, you'll be a lot happier when you finally say, "Your will be done" and open your clenched fist. But you'll never know until you let go.

C. S. Lewis said there are two kinds of people in the world, and only two kinds: those who say to God, "Your will be done" and those to whom God says in the end, "Your will be done." Which kind are you?

A Simple Prayer

Here's a simple prayer that may help you loosen your grip on the things with which you are struggling:

> *O Lord, Your will be done—*
> *nothing more,*
> *nothing less,*
> *nothing else.*
> *Amen.*

As always, we who pray that prayer are called by God to be part of the answer. We are to pray, "Your will be done," and then we are to see that God's will *is* done in our own lives.

> *Your will be done . . .*
> *in my life*
> *in my family*
> *in my finances*
> *in my career*
> *in my children*

in my dreams for the future
in my words
in my friendships
in my world.

When we pray that way, God will always be pleased to answer us. The answer may not be what we want or what we expect, but the answer *will* come, and we will not regret having asked. And best of all, when we pray that way, we are doing our little part to make the earth a little more like heaven and a little less like hell.

QUESTIONS FOR PERSONAL/GROUP STUDY

1. Have you ever faced a moment so desperate that you felt you couldn't pray? Can you think of a time when you were afraid to pray, "Your will be done" because you feared God's answer? Describe your experience and God's response.

2. What does it mean to say that God's will is rarely done on the earth? Explain your answer.

3. Why do you think God chose Dave Dravecky to go through such an ordeal? What does his example say to you?

4. Did Jesus lack confidence in God when he prayed in Gethsemane? If the answer is no, then what is the meaning of "If it be your will, let this cup pass from me"?

5. How do you feel about the statement, "God does not accept the status quo"? In what sense is the prayer "Your will be done" an act of God-ordained rebellion against the evil of this world?

6. What happens to the person who refuses to pray, "Your will be done"?

GOING DEEPER

When you pray, "Your will be done," you are asking that your life pass from your control to God's control. Think about the last twenty-four hours. Who has been in charge—you or the Lord? What are the signs that you are trying to control your own life? Circle the words that apply to you: irritable, pushy, anxious, fearful, angry, hyperactive, withdrawn, driven, compulsive, critical, hypersensitive, perfectionistic, overbearing, worried. Spend some time asking God to set you free from the need to always be in control.

FIERY TRIALS

On April 5, 1943, Dietrich Bonhoeffer was arrested and imprisoned by the Gestapo for his resistance to the Nazi regime in Germany. For several years he had spoken out against the Nazis, and eventually it caught up with him. As he saw his country sliding into the abyss, he felt that he could not remain silent. Two years later, only a few weeks before the end of World War II, he found himself in Buchenwald Concentration Camp, facing the death sentence. On Sunday, April 8, he led a service for other prisoners. Shortly after the final prayer, the door opened, and two civilians entered. "Prisoner Bonhoeffer, come with us," they said.

Everyone knew what that meant—the gallows. Quickly the other men said good-bye to him. An English prisoner who survived the war describes the moment: "He took me aside [and said], 'This is the end; but for me it is the beginning of life.'" The next day he was hanged at Flossenburg Prison. The SS doctor who witnessed his death called him brave and composed and devout to the very end. "Through the half-open door I saw Pastor Bonhoeffer still in his prison clothes, kneeling in fervent prayer to the Lord his God. The devotion and evident conviction of being heard that I saw in the prayer of this intensely captivating man moved me to the depths."

"This is the end; but for me it is the beginning of life." What makes a man facing certain death talk like that? Where do you find faith like that? Such a man has discovered the "living hope" (1 Peter 1:3) that goes beyond the grave. How else can you explain it?

WHY GOD SENDS TRIALS

British journalist Malcolm Muggeridge, who became a Christian before his death, said late in life, "Contrary to what might be expected, I look back on experiences that at the time seemed especially desolating and painful with particular satisfaction. Indeed, everything I have learned, everything that has truly enhanced and enlightened my existence, has been through affliction and not through happiness."

Every thoughtful person has wondered why God sends trials to his children. You don't live very long before that question stares you in the face. It might be a critical illness, the death of a loved one, loss of a job, the breakup of a marriage, trouble with your children, a season of depression, financial difficulties, or a time of intense persecution from others because of your faith. Those things happen to all of us sooner or later. If you've never pondered why God allows such things, you ought to.

When we turn to the Bible, we find many perspectives that help us understand why trials come to God's children. First Peter 1:6-7 offers an important insight that we need to know: "In this you rejoice, though now for a little while, if necessary, you have been grieved by various trials, so that the tested genuineness of your faith—more precious than gold that perishes though it is tested by fire—may be found to result in praise and glory and honor at the revelation of Jesus Christ." This passage doesn't answer every question we could ask about trials, troubles, and the sufferings of this life. No single text could do that. But it does provide a crucial framework for seeing the hand of God at work in the worst moments of life.

Before we jump into the text, let's notice two key words. The first is the word "trials" at the end of verse 6. The Greek word is *peirasmos*, a word that appears often in the New Testament. It can mean "test" or "trial" or even "temptation." Depending on the context, it can have a positive or negative connotation. When we face a test in school, we either pass or fail. The same is true of the tests of life. *God sends those tests so that what is in the heart will be revealed for all to see.* The same event may be both a test and a temptation. That is, it may be sent by God to test us, and Satan may use it as an occasion for temptation. It all depends on how we respond.

When trouble comes . . .

• We may turn to God in prayer, or we may become bitter.

• We may become quiet and thoughtful, or we may begin to complain.

• We may become tender and compassionate, or we may become harsh and cruel.

• We may learn new trust in God, or we may rebel against him.

• We may take courage, or we may give in to fear.

• We may draw close to God, or we may turn away from him.

It is the same event in all cases—but with vastly different results. It all depends on how we respond.

The second word comes from the first phrase of verse 6: "In this you rejoice." Take the root word *joy* and consider it for a moment. What is joy? It's a difficult word to define. We know that joy and happiness are two different things. Happiness depends on circumstances and comes and goes depending on the emotions of the moment. But joy is deeper and more profound because it comes from God. Last night as I pondered the matter, this thought came to me: Joy comes from satisfaction with God. When we are satisfied with God, we will have joy even in the hardest moments of life. G. K. Chesterton called joy "the gigantic secret of the Christian life." Joy, he said, is always at the center for the Christian; trials are at the periphery of life. I put these ideas together this way: *Joy is the ability to face reality—the good and bad, the happy and the sad, the positive and the negative, the best and the worst—because we are satisfied with God.*

Seen in that light, there is no contradiction between joy and trials. They belong together.

First Peter 1:6-7 teaches us four important truths about the trials of life.

Truth #1:
Our trials are brief

Peter begins by assuring his readers that their trials would only last "a little while" (v. 6). Of course, that "little while" seems to last forever when we are in the furnace. Early one Sunday morning when I asked a man how things were going, he shook his head and said, "Things are falling apart." I told him that he should listen closely to my sermon because I was preaching on how our trials are brief. He chuckled and said, "They don't seem brief to me." We all understand that. When you sit by the bedside of a loved one in the hospital, time seems to slow to a crawl. When your marriage crumbles or your children are in trouble or you lose your job and can't pay your bills, the trial seems to go on forever. In what sense can Peter say that our trials are brief?

The answer is, everything in this life is brief when compared to eternity. It's all a matter of perspective. If I say I know a man who can hold his breath a long time, I mean he can hold it for two or three minutes. That's a long time for breath-holding. But if someone says, "Pastor Ray, you've been at Calvary a long time," that person means that I've been here for fifteen years. That's a long time for a pastor to be at one church these days. Our trials may last for weeks or months or years, and sometimes they even last for decades; but seen against the endless ages of eternity, even the worst trials here are brief by comparison. Our problem is a kind of spiritual nearsightedness that views this world as the "real" world and counts eternity as nothing by comparison. God never asks us to deny the harsh reality of our trials. He asks only that we take his perspective on our suffering.

A wise pastor friend of mine wrote recently to say that his responsibility is not just to help people live well but to help them live with the great expectancy of heaven. "It is to prepare them to die well, even with excitement toward heaven and not regret." He went on to speak of a man who died while a pacemaker was being installed because the doctor clipped an artery without knowing it. The man had been in good health, but suddenly his life was over. It all changed with one prick of a wire. My friend said that he thinks about this more often now because he is fifty, and he is seeing friends his age (and younger) beginning to die.

When we are young, death seems rather theoretical; and even when it happens, it seems remote from our own experience. But time has a way of changing our thinking. My friend spoke of a nine-year-old boy in his congregation who has a cancerous tumor in his brain. Chemo didn't work, and he faces radiation soon. His vision is going quickly. "Every time I see him or think of him, I realize my ministry to him, unless the Lord intervenes, is to help him die with joy and anticipation of Christ. And it is to help the parents understand that his life cut short is not loss but gain." My friend speaks words that come from the heart of God. Life is short for all of us compared to eternity. And in the worst of our trials, we can rejoice because we know they will not, they cannot last forever.

Truth #2:
Our trials are necessary

Note how Peter puts it: "If necessary, you have been grieved by various trials." Literally, the Greek reads, "If necessary for a little while." Peter cannot be sure how long they would suffer, but he knows that the suffering itself is necessary. Whether long or short, hard times come to every believer. Those hard times come in many varieties. (When I said that one Sunday morning, a voice from the back of the sanctuary said, "Amen!") And they come over and over again. And those hard times come to every believer. No Christian is exempt from trials. Some have more, others less, but all share in the "various trials" Peter mentions. Those trials are necessary to help us grow spiritually. That's why Martin Luther called adversity "the very best book in my library." And George Whitefield declared, "God puts burs in our bed to keep us watchful and awake." Perhaps that is why you could not sleep last night. Those trials are proof that we belong to the Lord.

As I write these words, my friend Catherine Faires is battling ovarian cancer. After the first round of treatment, the cancer seemed to go into remission. Several months later, the doctors told her it had come back again. She has been keeping her friends informed about her situation through e-mail. After reading her most recent update, I spoke with her on the phone, and she gave me permission to share what she wrote. "If my story can help others and bring glory to God, that's what I want." This is part of what she wrote to her friends:

> The other day I was listening to the radio and heard a song by Avalon called "Testify to Love." My church sometimes sings it as part of worship. I suddenly saw this line, "As long as I shall live, I will testify to love" from a new perspective. With recurrent, metastatic ovarian cancer, the statistics give me six to eight months to live. I know that "As long as I shall live" isn't going to be very long (unless God intervenes) and it makes the line all the more powerful for me.
>
> With whatever time and breath I have left, I will testify to what God has done for me and who God is to me. Oh, I forgot to tell you that I think "love" is wishy-washy so I change it to "God" when I'm singing along with the radio. I mean, there are so many kinds of "love" and I want to be clear about what I mean. On second thought, there are several understandings of

"God" so maybe I need to specify "the God of the Bible" but that would mess with the rhythm. . . .

So here is what God has done for me recently: God gave me a Christian nurse in the hospital yesterday who encouraged me with her testimony of God's work in her life. God gives me good friends who call and visit me in the hospital. God has used this illness to put me back in touch with friends from grad school that I'd lost contact with over the years. Since my church's women's retreat this spring, I've been reminded that God is my first love, so I write my journals to "my love," and that is making the idea of dying a lot less scary.

Praise God for all these gifts from his hand. Praise God for my participation in the State University Retirement System (SURS) that is providing me with disability checks and an excellent health insurance program. Please continue to pray for my body to respond to the new drug, although I'd rather my hair didn't respond by falling out (a likely side effect). Please pray for the Holy Spirit to fill and use me to testify about my Lord.

Thank you, each and every one.

Catherine

I submit to you that Catherine Faires is living proof that you can trust God even when your life hangs in the balance. It is only by God's grace that in the midst of this fiery trial she can write like this.

Truth #3:
Our trials are purifying

We have arrived at the heart of Peter's message. Trials come "so that the tested genuineness of your faith—more precious than gold that perishes though it is tested by fire" (v. 7) may be seen by everyone. Note the little phrase "so that" in the text. Circle it, underline it, highlight it. No phrase is more hopeful or more needed. *The words "so that" tell us that our trials have a purpose.* They don't just happen by chance or by some random act of fate. There are no accidents for the children of God. Everything happens for a reason. Even though we may not see the reason, our faith can survive if we know that a divine purpose really does exist.

Peter goes on to explain that God sends trials in order to test and purify our faith. The phrase "tested genuineness" translates a Greek word that means to test something in order to prove that it will not fail. Let me illustrate. When Chevrolet tests Ford pickup trucks, they do it to prove that Ford trucks won't pass the test. But when Chevrolet tests its own trucks, they do it to prove that their trucks will pass the same test. That's the Greek word used here. *God puts our faith to the test by allowing hard times to come—not to destroy us but to demonstrate that our faith is genuine.* Note the contrast between faith and pure gold. Did you know that it takes four tons of gold ore to produce one ounce of pure gold? During the refining process, the gold ore is heated in a giant furnace until it liquefies; the dross or waste material is skimmed off, leaving only the pure gold at the bottom.

In ancient times goldsmiths knew they had pure gold when they could look at the gold and see their reflection. That's what God intends through our trials. He puts us in the furnace to burn off the greed, the impatience, the unkindness, the anger, the bitterness, the hatred, the lust, and the selfishness. For most of us, that's a lifetime process. But in the end, the image of Jesus is formed in us. I have seen that happen over and over again in the lives of suffering saints. "Joe, you look like Jesus to me." "Sandra, I can see Jesus in your face."

God wants to prove your faith is genuine, and trials provide the most reliable proof. We may all mouth certain phrases that make us sound spiritual when things are going well, but how we respond when life tumbles in around us tells the real story of what we truly believe. God "proves" our faith to us, to our loved ones, and to a watching world. Outside the four walls of the church are millions of people who watch the way we live. They may not understand what we believe, but they watch us from a distance to see how we respond when hard times come. And even if they don't understand it all, they are profoundly moved by a believer whose faith remains strong in the time of trouble. They know our faith is real, and that draws them one step closer to Jesus.

This is how it works:

• You lost your money but gained devoted faith.
• You lost your health but gained patient faith.
• You lost your job but gained resilient faith.
• You lost your loved ones but gained grieving faith.
• You lost your friends but gained courageous faith.

In this way God brings triumph out of our trials. From the pit of despair, he lifts us to the pinnacle of faith. Hard times make strong saints. There is no other way.

Truth #4:
Our trials are eternally significant

Our text suggests one final truth about our trials. God sends trials to prove our faith is genuine so that it "may be found to result in praise and glory and honor at the revelation of Jesus Christ" (v. 7). Normally when we read words like praise, glory, and honor, we associate them with Jesus Christ himself. But Peter says we are the ones who gain praise, glory, and honor. That is, the Lord himself bestows upon us praise and glory and honor. Or more properly, because of our faithfulness during our trials in this life, we will share in the praise, glory, and honor that belong to our Lord. What a thought that is. What an incredible scene in heaven, when the faithful saints of God are crowned with glory, praise, and honor by our Lord himself. I imagine Jesus saying, "Father, this is Mario. He suffered for my sake on the earth, and he never denied my name. He is one of my faithful ones." As those words are spoken, a vast cheer rolls across the universe from the assembled multitudes. And so it will go as one by one those who suffered so much in this life, those who endured ridicule, hatred, and martyrdom, are revealed and rewarded for their faithfulness. In the same way those who suffered illness with joy, who lost their possessions but not their faith, who walked a hard road on the earth but never gave up will be recognized and honored by the Lord.

When Jesus finally appears, we will find out what our trials have accomplished. Things that seemed useless and unfair will be seen as instruments of God's grace. Things we thought were hard and even cruel, we will discover were tempered by God's mercy.

And we will all say,

- "He was nearest when I thought him farthest away."
- "He was faithful when I had no faith to believe."
- "He used my trials to develop my faith."
- "He used my faith to encourage others."

We don't see those things very clearly now, but in that day, all will be made plain. And as we look back across the pathway of life, we will see that nothing was wasted. God knew what he was doing all along.

THREE FINAL THOUGHTS

Before we wrap up this message, here are three concluding thoughts about the troubles of life that we all face sooner or later.

Trouble is something we should expect.

After what our Lord endured two thousand years ago, how can we ever say, "I can't believe this is happening to me!" It is much better to face the trials of life with wide-eyed realism, understanding that suffering is the first course in God's curriculum in the School of Spiritual Growth.

Trouble is meant to draw us closer to the Lord, not to push us farther away.

Strange as it may seem, our troubles are a sign of God's love, for if he did not love us, he would not discipline us (see Hebrews

12:4-11). Some of you may say, "If that's the case, then God must love me *a lot*." I am certain that he does, and your trials and your tears and the confusion you experience do not invalidate his love for you. C. S. Lewis remarked that God whispers to us in our pleasure but shouts to us in our pain. He called pain "God's megaphone" to rouse a sleeping world. Many times God speaks to us through our pain because we won't listen to him any other way.

Trouble is meant to be used and not wasted.

Our hard times are not easy, and sometimes they are not good at all, but God can use them for our good and for his glory. He intends to prove our faith genuine by the way we respond to our trials. Think of it this way:

• Before our trials, our faith is *unproved*.
• After our trials, our faith is *improved*.

A faith that God approves brings him great glory. Here is good news for all of us.

• God is not looking for educated people.
• God is not looking for rich people.
• God is not looking for talented people.
• God is not looking for beautiful people.
• God is looking for faithful disciples who, having passed through the fiery trials, are stamped for all the world to see: "Approved by God."

As I write these words, I am sure that some of you are going through incredibly difficult situations at this very moment. What is God saying to you?

• It will not last forever.
• It is necessary for your spiritual growth.
• It is sent to help you, not to hurt you.

If you find yourself in the furnace right now, be of good cheer. *It is your Father's kindness that has put you there.* One Sunday a man told me that he is being "barbecued" by what he is going through. But he did not seem angry at all. He knows that the pain is helping him grow and become a new man by God's grace. *Nothing of value will be taken while you are in the furnace.* The only things taken from you will be those things you didn't need anyway.

JOY AND TRIALS

And so I come back to the two words I mentioned at the beginning of this chapter: *trials* and *joy*. Now we can see clearly how these two always work together.

The Christian position is not joy, then trials, and it is not trials, then joy.

It is always joy and trials, at the same time, working together, mixed together, so that we have joy in our trials, joy beside our trials, joy within our trials, and sometimes even joy in spite of our trials. Thus David could say in Psalm 34:8, after mentioning his fears and his troubles, "Oh, taste and see that the LORD is good!" Indeed, his mercies endure forever, but most of us only discover that truth in the furnace. Jesus comes to us in our time of direst need, and just when we need him most, he is there.

When hard times come, this is what we must say:

• Whatever it takes, Lord, do your work in me.
• Whatever it takes to purify my heart, do your work in me.
• Whatever it takes to build my faith, do your work in me.
• Whatever it takes to make me like Jesus, do your work in me.
• If that means doing some "furnace time," do your work in me.
• If that means fiery trials today and more tomorrow, do your work in me.
• Lord, I want my life to be approved by you; so do your work in me.

This is God's call to all of us. *Embrace the cross that God is calling you to bear.* Stop fighting with God. Stop complaining. Stop blaming others. *And open your heart to exceeding great joy.* Some of us have never discovered this kind of joy because we fight God at the point of our trials. But joy and trials come together in God's plan. There is no exceedingly great joy without the suffering that goes with it. Don't fear the cost of great rejoicing. Humble yourself under the mighty hand of God. Do not resist his work in your life, and he will lift you up.

QUESTIONS FOR PERSONAL/GROUP STUDY

1. What difference does it make to someone dying of cancer to know that our suffering is temporary? Is it a cop-out to say such a thing since suffering for some people won't end until they get to heaven?

2. Why is hope such an important part of the Christian response to suffering? Write down at least three reasons why a Christian can have hope even in the midst of great personal difficulty.

3. How would your life be changed if you came to regard your struggles as gifts from God meant for your benefit rather than as burdens to be carried or punishments to be endured?

4. Take a look at your prayer list, and pick out the toughest circumstance you face. Spend some time thanking God that his Holy Spirit is at work in that situation in ways you can't even imagine. Ask God to give you grace to patiently wait for his answer.

5. Malcolm Muggeridge says that we learn more through suffering than through happiness. Why is this so?

6. What obstacles stand in the way of your embracing the seven statements at the end of this chapter? Are you willing to ask God to remove those obstacles and embrace his work in your life?

GOING DEEPER

One popular view today says that suffering is never God's will for the Christian. Some go so far as to suggest that accepting suffering is a sub-Christian view that dishonors God, who wants his children to always enjoy health, wealth, and prosperity. How would you respond to that view? Make a list of the people you've known whose faith has grown stronger through the suffering they have endured.

FAITHFUL IN THE FURNACE

The word *martyr* has the sound of antiquity about it. It's a word that belongs to the days of Jesus and the apostles, and to the persecuted early Christians who were thrown to the lions in Rome. A few of us have read in *Foxe's Book of Martyrs* about the persecution of God's children across the centuries. And perhaps we have heard about the terrible suffering in the Sudan where Christians are being kidnapped and sold into slavery. For most of us the word *martyr* belongs to another time and another place. It seems rather remote from where we live today. If we think that, we are wrong. More Christians were killed for their faith in the last century than in all previous centuries combined.

That leads me to ask a simple question: Could such a thing ever happen today where we live? Could any of us ever be called upon to pay the ultimate price for our faith? No less an authority than Robert Coleman, author of *The Master Plan of Evangelism* and a professor at Gordon-Conwell Theological Seminary, says the answer is yes. He sees suffering ahead for the church in the West. He notes, "It's when the night closes in that we see the stars. God loves us too much to leave us in our complacency" (quoted by John H. Armstrong in his article "Faithful Witness: The Relationship of Persecution to Our Faith, Part I," in *Viewpoint*, January-February 2000, Volume 4, Number 1, p.

11). I think Coleman is right. Our day of complacency will come to an end soon. I don't think there is serious doubt about this. Our culture is fading, and the freedoms we have enjoyed may pass with it.

One has only to think of the controversy surrounding gay marriage. The greatest problem we face is not "out there," it's "in here," inside the evangelical church where we have suffered a profound loss of nerve. I attended a banquet (Christian Booksellers Association Convention, 2004) that featured a film clip of the late Francis Schaeffer talking about the importance of standing for the truth in an age of personal peace and affluence. I was reminded again how great a prophet he really was. He said that at such a time our only concern is often ourselves and our family. He predicted in the mid-seventies that the unthinkable would become thinkable and even acceptable in our society. His words have come true in our day.

Then there was a brief clip of Edith Schaeffer who is now ninety years old. In a slow, clear voice she said, "The only thing that matters is truth." She's right about that. *Truth matters.* That's why we need to know what God says. I know we live in an anti-intellectual age, but truth matters. I realize that in the evangelical movement we have elevated personal experience almost to the level of Scripture itself, but truth matters. Truth towers over our personal experience and stands in judgment over our personal opinions. The current debate over same-sex marriage is a case in point. Some church members would prefer that their pastor not say anything about such a volatile issue. Although we have the truth that sets people free, we're afraid to share it for fear that some will be offended. That's what I mean by a profound loss of nerve.

To say, "Thus says the Lord" in our pluralistic society, to declare that there is only one way to God, is to risk not only public ridicule but also open hostility. The day may not be far away when witnessing for Christ to your classmates or coworkers or neighbors will be considered a hate crime. And what will we do then?

In our day many Christians are praying fervently for revival in the American church. What would happen if God did revive us? John Armstrong answers this way:

> I am personally convinced, the longer I ponder this question, that we should expect a general increase in suffering if God were to grant us a true awakening. Such a move of God would, by definition, equip the church to face days of amazing spiritual opportunity. I also think it is becoming increasingly obvious that such opportunity would also be linked with incredible personal difficulty! ("Faithful Witness: The Relationship of Persecution to Our Faith, Part I")

Perhaps you've heard of Tertullian, the famous second-century lawyer who was converted by watching Christians sing as they marched to their deaths. No wonder he gave us this famous statement: "The blood of the martyrs is the seed of the church." St. Augustine wrote, "The martyrs were bound, jailed, scourged, wracked, burned, rent, butchered—and they multiplied."

The suffering of the faithful is still part of God's plan. That is no less true today than in the second century. And it was true in Daniel's day when Shadrach, Meshach, and Abednego stood before mighty King Nebuchadnezzar. When that monarch ordered all his leaders to bow down before the golden image, those three Hebrews—and they alone—refused. When called to give an account of their disobedience, they replied that the king could do what he wanted, but their God could deliver them, and even if he didn't, no matter what happened to them, they would not bow down.

Their heroic words speak across the centuries to us today. Let's consider what they said and what it means for us in the twenty-first century. I urge you to pay close attention. You may need this truth sooner than you think.

AN ABSOLUTE CONVICTION

"Our God whom we serve is able to deliver us from the burning fiery furnace" (Daniel 3:17a). This might be called Applied Theology 101. They did not doubt the king's intention to throw them into the blazing furnace. They didn't doubt his ability or his willingness to act if necessary. I am sure they had seen firsthand how cruel he could be to anyone who crossed him.

What gave them the confidence to speak so boldly? Three little words: "*God . . . is able.*" What a thought this is. They knew their God, and they knew what he could do.

God is able to deliver! God is able to save! God is able to rescue! And how did they know that? They remembered what he had done in the past.

• He spoke, and the stars flew into the skies.

• He spoke, and the planets began spinning around the sun.

• He spoke, and the lion roared, and the eagle soared, and the fish began to swim.

• He took a lump of clay and made a man.

• Then he took the man's rib and made a woman.

• He turned a rod into a serpent and back into a rod again.

• He sent a wind, and the Red Sea parted.

• He set a table in the wilderness and fed his children manna and quail.

• He brought forth water from a rock.

• He caused the walls of Jericho to come tumblin' down.

Shadrach, Meshach, and Abednego had been taught these stories since they were tiny children. Because they knew their God, they knew what he could do. Therefore, in their own time of crisis, they knew beyond any shadow of doubt that God is able.

Let me say it plainly. Because they knew what God had done

in the past, they knew what he could do in the present. This is the great value that comes from learning God's Word. You discover who God is, what he has done, and what he can do. Knowing God gives you the strength to stand your ground no matter who is standing against you.

A Strong Hope

"He will deliver us out of your hand, O king" (Daniel 3:17b). There was a strong note of optimism in their voices as they stood before the mightiest man in the world. The fiery furnace was not too many yards away, certainly within eyesight, I would think. They knew the price for disobedience, but they disobeyed anyway. Why? Because they believed deep in their souls that somehow, some way God would rescue them. They expected some kind of deliverance. They didn't know how or what or where or when.

Now what made them talk like this? I answer very simply. *They had a big God.* They believed in a God who could do anything. That's why Hebrews 11:34 refers to them when it says, "quenched the fury of the flames" (NIV). Here is strong optimism at a time when hope seemed gone.

As I wrote those words my mind went back to a day thirty years ago when I was just married and newly enrolled as a first-year student at Dallas Theological Seminary. A month or so into the first semester my mom called with the bad news that my father was sick and had been taken to the hospital in Birmingham, Alabama. We made a quick trip, saw my father, and then returned to Dallas. (I realize that I shared parts of this experience earlier in this book, but I want to make a different point here.) A few days later my mom called again and said we'd better come back to Birmingham as quickly as possible. So we packed our bags, hopped in our little green 1974 Ford Pinto, and headed for the airport. I seem to recall that there wasn't much traffic that day.

As we drove north on Central Expressway I saw a billboard sponsored by a stock brokerage firm. It featured a digital read-out showing the change in the Dow Jones average. Since it was the weekend, there were no figures to quote. The sign read, "+0.00." Plus zero. That seemed to be a good way to summarize my faith at that moment. My father was gravely ill (and would eventually die), but we were going back with as much faith as we could muster.

That's where those three young men were. Humanly speaking, their chances of survival were zero. *But because of God, at least it was plus zero.* Many of you stand in that same spot. The circumstances seem stacked against you. But because of God, you can always be at plus zero. That's a lot better than minus zero, which is where you are when you don't know God at all.

AN UNWAVERING RESOLVE

"But if not, be it known to you, O king, that we will not serve your gods or worship the golden image that you have set up" (Daniel 3:18). And so we come to the most powerful words of all. There are various stages in the life of faith, and this may be the highest. Here they were saying, "We know God can deliver us, but we don't know if he will deliver us. But either way, we won't bow down before your golden image." Basically they were signing their own death warrant, and they knew it. How many of us would have that kind of courage?

This was God's Moral Minority. They knew it was better to die a thousand times with God's approval than to live one day without it. Better a fiery furnace than to live with the fire of a guilty conscience burning in your soul. They could die, but they dare not sin! Their convictions were not for sale. Not at any price, not even their own lives.

What a noble example of faith. They hoped for a miracle, but they didn't demand one. They left everything in the hands of God!

Consider that little phrase: "but if not."

• We want our prayers answered—but if not . . .
• We want long life and good health—but if not . . .
• We want our children to prosper—but if not . . .
• We want to see miracles happen—but if not . . .

If God says no to your cherished dreams and your fondest hopes, will you still trust him? If God says no to your plans for the future, will you still serve him? If God says no when through your tears you pray for those you love, will you still follow him?

This brings us face to face with a doctrine we don't talk about very much: *the unpredictability of God*. That means God does what he wants to do, not what we expect him to do. These three young men had a big God, and they knew that their personal deliverance might not be the most important thing to him. That's a key insight because for most of us, when we get in a tight place the only thing we can think about is making sure we get out okay. So when we pray, we say, "O Lord, please get me out of this jam." Sometimes we even say, "If it be your will." But we don't say that very loudly because we hope God's will is the same as ours.

But often it isn't. We see through a glass darkly. At best we see only a glimmer of God's purposes, like peeking through a pinhole. But God sees the whole panorama of history stretched out before him.

UNANSWERED QUESTIONS

There are so many mysteries in life. Deuteronomy 29:29 tells us that "the secret things belong to the LORD our God," which means he knows why everything happens, but he's not telling anyone else. Consider these mysteries: In Acts 12 the apostle James was killed with the sword; in the same chapter the apostle Peter was miraculously delivered. Why? Hezekiah asked for and was given fifteen more years of life; yet Rachel died in childbirth on her way to Bethlehem. Why?

One man gets cancer and dies at forty-two; another lives to be eighty-five. Why?

One child does well, and another struggles all his life. Why?

One family knows prosperity and seems to have it made, while another can barely make ends meet. Why?

Your friend is promoted, and you are passed over, though you do better work. Why?

One man dies while working out, while a little girl is run over by a car and jumps up with nothing but a few bruises. Why?

Two soldiers go to war; only one comes home. Why?

One child is born healthy, another with serious physical disabilities. Why?

Some prayers are answered; others apparently are never answered. Why?

The list could be extended to infinity. There are so many mysteries in the universe. *None have clear answers.* In the end there is only one answer. I call it The First Rule of the Spiritual Life: He's God and we're not! Psalm 115:3 reminds us, "Our God is in the heavens; he does all that he pleases."

What we find in Daniel 3 is faith in God, not just faith in God's deliverance. These young men were saying, "We are sure of God, but we are not sure what God will do." No prosperity theology here.

THE OTHER SIDE OF FAITH

Earlier in this chapter I quoted Hebrews 11:34. But there is more to the story than that. If I left the matter there, I would be leaving a very incomplete picture. It sounds too easy. Living by faith is often very difficult. And it doesn't always end up the way we would like.

Suppose we ask the question this way: Does living by faith mean you will always receive a miracle? *The answer must be no.* The end of Hebrews 11 makes that very clear. Verses 33-35a record The Triumphs of Faith:

Who through faith conquered kingdoms, enforced justice, obtained promises, stopped the mouths of lions, quenched the power of fire, escaped the edge of the sword, were made strong out of weakness, became mighty in war, put foreign armies to flight. Women received back their dead by resurrection.

That's a wonderful list, and we can all think of the great biblical heroes who did these things. But that is only part of the story. Verses 35b-38 record The Trials of Faith:

Some were tortured, refusing to accept release, so that they might rise again to a better life. Others suffered mocking and flogging, and even chains and imprisonment. They were stoned, they were sawn in two, they were killed with the sword. They went about in skins of sheep and goats, destitute, afflicted, mistreated—of whom the world was not worthy—wandering about in deserts and mountains, and in dens and caves of the earth.

Who were these poor, benighted souls? What had they done to deserve such punishment? The writer simply calls them "some" and "others." They were "others" who lived by faith. *These men and women who endured such torment were living by faith just as much as Noah, Abraham, Moses, or Joshua.* Their faith was not weaker. If anything, their faith was stronger because it enabled them to endure incredible suffering. They were not lesser saints because they found no miracle. If anything, they were greater saints because they were faithful even when things didn't work out right.

EVEN UNTIL DEATH

Early in my ministry at Calvary Memorial Church in Oak Park, Illinois, I preached a series of sermons on our Church Covenant. Like most churches, we hardly ever mention our Church Covenant, and I discovered that most people didn't know we had one. That covenant describes the kind of commitments people are making to each other and to the Lord when they join the church. Here is one part of our Church Covenant: "We do, therefore, in his strength promise . . . that we will in all conditions, even unto death, strive to live to the glory of Him who has called us out of darkness into His marvelous light."

The last part is clear. *We are to live to the glory of God.* But the phrase "in all conditions" sounds like Hebrews 11. And the phrase "even until death" sounds like the "others" in 11:35-38. Did the writers of our Church Covenant really expect us to take that seriously? Are we promising to be faithful even unto death? I think the answer must be yes. We hope it never comes to that. We pray that it doesn't. But it might.

THE TRIUMPH OF KAREN WATSON

Karen Watson of Bakersfield, California, trusted Christ as her Savior in 1997 after a period of intense personal grief. Her boyfriend whom she had planned to marry, her father, and her grandmother all died within a two-year span. After coming to Christ, she joined others from her local church on short-term missions trips. She went twice to El Salvador and once to Kosovo, Macedonia, and Greece. Eventually she felt God calling her to full-time service; so she resigned her job as a detention officer in the sheriff's department in Bakersfield, sold her car and her house, and joined the International Mission Board of the Southern Baptist Convention. She packed all her worldly possessions in a single duffel bag. Because she was a natural leader, she was asked to coordinate refugee work in Jordan during the war in Iraq. Soon after major combat ended, she was assigned to Iraq itself. Though she was fully aware of the dangers, she did not hesitate to obey the call.

On March 15, 2004, she and four other missionaries were in the northern Iraqi city of Mosul when they were attacked in a drive-by shooting. The assailants fired automatic weapons and rocket-powered grenades. Four of the missionaries died; one was critically injured. Karen Watson, thirty-eight, was among the dead.

Before she went to Iraq, she gave her pastor a handwritten letter to be opened only on the event of her death. This is what she wrote (as printed in *Baptist Press News*, March 24, 2004):

March 7, 2003
Dear Pastor Phil & Pastor Roger,

You should only be opening this letter in the event of death.

When God calls there are no regrets. I tried to share my heart with you as much as possible, my heart for the Nations. I wasn't called to a place. I was called to Him. To obey was my objective, to suffer was expected, His glory was my reward, His glory is my reward.

One of the most important things to remember right now is to preserve the work. . . . I am writing this as if I am still working among my people group.

I thank you all so much for your prayers and support. Surely your reward in Heaven will be great. Thank you for investing in my life and spiritual well being. Keep sending missionaries out. Keep raising up fine young pastors.

In regards to any service, keep it small and simple. Yes simple, just preach the gospel. . . . Be bold and preach the life saving, life changing, forever eternal GOSPEL. Give glory and honor to our Father.

The Missionary Heart:
Care more than some think is wise.
Risk more than some think is safe.
Dream more than some think is practical.
Expect more than some think is possible.

I was called not to comfort or success but to obedience. . . .

There is no Joy outside of knowing Jesus and serving Him.

I love you two and my church family.

In His care,
Salaam, Karen

At her funeral, Pastor Roger Spradlin asked, "Does it pay to serve God . . . [when] kindness is greeted by a hail of bullets?" Then he gave the answer: "It pays if you value the attention of God more than the approval of men. It pays if you value others more than yourself. If we were to ask Karen, she would say, 'Oh yes!'"

Three little words echo across the years, from the plains of Dura in ancient Babylon to a city in northern Iraq to wherever you happen to be as you read this book: "But if not . . ."

We all hope and pray to live long lives in peace and safety. No one wants to be a martyr for Christ. But the days may be coming, and perhaps are not that faraway, when some of us may be called upon to make the ultimate choice.

In all these things we have the Word of God as our hope and strength. Fear not; trust in him. Our God is able to deliver us. But if not, may we be found faithful to Christ, even unto death.

QUESTIONS FOR PERSONAL/GROUP STUDY

1. Read Daniel 3. What excuses could the three young men have given for bowing down to the golden statue?

2. "It's when the night closes in that we see the stars. God loves us too much to leave us in our complacency." In what ways can persecution and opposition because of our faith be a sign of God's love for us?

3. Can you think of any ways in which you have suffered personally or professionally because of your faith in Christ?

4. If God is able to save us from suffering, why doesn't he always do it?

5. How can a good memory help you in times of trouble?

6. How have you experienced the "unpredictability of God"?

GOING DEEPER

Most of us will never do what Karen Watson did by going into a war zone in the name of Christ. But all of us can leave behind a written legacy of our faith. Here's the challenge. Write a letter to your loved ones that is not to be opened until after your death. What would you like to say to your family and friends? How will you express your faith in Jesus Christ? What are the values you want to pass on? Write the letter, and then put it in a safe place. Someday it may be your final legacy to those you leave behind.

SHOW ME YOUR GLORY

M oses said, 'Please show me your glory'" (Exodus 33:18).
Charles Spurgeon calls this the greatest request a man ever
made of God. I think he is right. How could Moses have asked
for anything larger? *To see God's glory is to see God himself.* It
was as if Moses were saying, "Let me see you as you really are."
Usually when men pray, they want some special favor from the
Lord. "Lord, help me find a job" or "Heal my child" or "Reveal
your will to me" or "Increase my faith" or "Save me from this
day of trouble." Those prayers are noble in themselves because
they ask God for what only God can give. If we ask that a mountain be cast into the sea, we are asking for something we ourselves
cannot do. So even our "ordinary" prayers honor the Lord
because they recognize that God is God and we are not.

But this prayer of Moses stands entirely alone. It is a category
unto itself. No other request can be compared to it. God's glory
is the sum total of who he is. It is God's power plus his wisdom
plus his justice plus his mercy plus his faithfulness plus his holiness plus his love plus every other attribute of his character. God's
glory is the shining forth of who God is in his essence.

*We can only understand this request if we consider the con-
text.* Moses had just spent forty days on Mount Sinai communing
with the Lord. During those days on the mountain, God revealed

his law to Moses and wrote the Ten Commandments on tablets of stone with his finger. While Moses was with the Lord, the children of Israel grew restless. So Aaron gathered gold earrings from the people and constructed a golden calf. They danced and shouted and proclaimed, "These are your gods, O Israel, who brought you up out of the land of Egypt!" (Exodus 32:4). The people offered sacrifices to the golden calf and began to engage in wild revelry. The Lord knew all about it and told Moses that he was going to destroy Israel and start over with a new nation that would worship him and not turn to idols.

But Moses interceded with the Lord for his stiff-necked, rebellious people. He reminded God of the promise he had made to Abraham, and he also said that the pagans would say he brought his people into the wilderness just to kill them. So the Lord relented and did not destroy the people.

Then Moses came down from the mountain. When he saw the people and their wild celebration, he threw down the stone tablets in anger. He burned the golden calf, ground it to power, mixed it with water, and made the Israelites drink it. Then he called for those who were still loyal to God to rally to his side. The Levites stood with him, and at his instruction they went through the camp killing the idolaters. Three thousand people died that day. The next day Moses pled with God for forgiveness for his people. He even asked God to blot his own name out of his book in order to save the people of Israel. God told him to lead the people away from Mt. Sinai and toward the Promised Land, but with one significant condition: "I will not go up among you, lest I consume you on the way, for you are a stiff-necked people" (Exodus 33:3).

This is our greatest fear—that when we go, the Lord will not go with us. *It happens more often than we think.* In our haste to get on with life, we take control of the situation, and the results do not work out as we'd hoped. I wonder how many of us can look back at some major decision and say, "I see now that the Lord wasn't in that at all. I did that one all by myself." The tragedy of going on without the Lord is that we generally don't discover it until it's too late to do much about it. Wrong decisions can't always be undone. So Moses interceded with God again. This time he said, "If you don't go with us, we're aren't going to go" (Exodus 33:15). That's the right attitude to have. If God has led you out of Egypt, you'd better not leave him behind at Mt. Sinai. You're going to need his help to navigate the wilderness.

Then comes the great request in verse 18—"Show me your glory." God's answer is a qualified yes. "I will show you my glory," he says in essence, "but not all of it." Moses would see God's goodness, but he would not see God's face, for no one can see God's face and live (Exodus 33:20). Then God offered to hide Moses in "a cleft of the rock" so Moses could see his back as he passed by. That is more than any man had ever seen before. That is the most Moses could see and not die.

Truth #1:
We discover God's glory in time of crisis

Moses prayed, "Show me your glory" only after the children of Israel began to worship the golden calf. And he prayed this way after he had broken the tablets of the Ten Commandments, and after three thousand Israelites had died, and after he had interceded with God several times. And this prayer came after he had saved the nation from destruction, and after he had received God's promise not to abandon his people. No doubt the ongoing crisis had drained much of Moses' natural strength. We all have our limits, don't we?

Tom Landry, longtime coach of the Dallas Cowboys, was fond of remarking, "Fatigue makes cowards of us all." *Most of us can handle a little bit of adversity, and some of us can handle a lot of adversity, but everyone has a breaking point. It* doesn't matter who you are or where you are or what your track record is. We all have a breaking point—and sometimes we discover it without warning. There is a lesson here if we care to learn it.

- You're not as strong as you think you are, and neither am I.
- You're not as wise as you think you are, and neither am I.
- You're not as clever as you think you are, and neither am I.
- You're not as self-sufficient as you think you are, and neither am I.

The mightiest oak tree in the forest looks invincible, but if you hit it in just the right place with a tiny axe, it comes crashing down. The axe may be small, but it can bring down a tree in just a few seconds. *It is a good thing that God sends us through fiery trials or else we would never see his glory.* I received an e-mail from a man in Pennsylvania who had read one of my books. Not long ago the doctors told him he has prostate cancer. In times past he had made many mistakes and had hurt his family greatly. "Difficult times. Tremendous guilt and pain. So when I got news of cancer I thought, 'I certainly deserve it.'" He obtained a copy of my book and took it with him to work. He said he works twelve-hour shifts and often goes onto rooftops to pray late at night.

> It was while reading your book that God and I came to peaceful terms with cancer. Not only that but he gave me ability to see how cancer would be useful in His kingdom and in my life. Cancer clears away the cobwebs, cancer clarifies, cancer makes concise, cancer enables you to find comfort in God and freedom from the world's entrapments.

If he had not had cancer, he would never have discovered these things. Cancer may not be good in and of itself, but it can be good to have cancer if out of that crisis you come to a new understanding of God.

We learn more in the darkness than we do in the light. We grow stronger in affliction than when the sun is shining and all is well. It is not coincidence that Moses discovered God's glory in a time of personal crisis. It will be the same for us as well.

Truth #2:
The revelation of God's glory
comes at a personal cost

God told Moses he would answer his prayer, but not in the way he expected. In a sense Moses had no idea what he was asking for. He wanted to see God's glory, but that meant seeing God in his essence. No man can see God's essence and live. The light would blind us, and then it would consume us. So God told Moses he would hide him in "a cleft of the rock" so he would see God's back as the Lord passed by. That alone would be overwhelming to Moses, but at least he would not die.

Sometimes when we pray, we ask for things that we cannot bear alone. We want certain blessings, but we have no idea of the cost involved. And certainly when we pray, "Lord, show me your glory," like Moses of old, we are asking for something that goes far beyond our limited abilities to receive. Several years ago our church adopted the theme, "Lord, teach us to pray." On the first Sunday of that year, I did something I had never done before. At the end of my sermon I asked the congregation to pray for me in a special way during the year. On the spur of the moment, I asked people not to come into the sanctuary unless they had prayed for me that day. I told them I felt my need for their prayers very deeply, and I begged them to pray for me.

Later I found out that my request for prayer unnerved certain people. They wondered if something was "wrong" in my life that caused me to ask for prayer. A few weeks later I repeated that request to the congregation. One lady came up and asked me why

I had chosen this particular year to ask for prayer. On the spur of the moment I replied, "I have no idea, but I'm sure it will be revealed eventually." That was in early February.

A few weeks later I traveled to a Bible conference in Florida to teach for a week. I wasn't feeling well when I arrived. I wasn't exactly sick, but I suppose you could say I was "off my oats" a bit. Just a touch under the weather. After I finished my final message, I went back to my room and more or less collapsed. It was as if my body said, "The work is done for the week, so now it's time to get sick." I just felt miserable, started running a fever, got the shakes—the whole nine yards. Marlene and I flew home later that day, but my condition didn't improve. The next day I got a bit worse. The whole thing baffled me since I'm in the category of people who "never get sick." I had been truly sick exactly once in thirty years. That was in 1986 when I contracted mononucleosis. I ended up not preaching for three Sundays because of it. But since then, I'd never missed a Sunday because of sickness.

But my record was about to be broken. Later that Saturday I developed a pain that made it difficult for me to stand up. The flu or whatever it was had morphed into some kind of infection. By that night I knew I was in a bit of trouble. Finally at 3:00 A.M. I realized that I wasn't going to be able to preach that morning. Later that day I started on a course of antibiotics that I hoped would help.

The next day I was mostly unchanged. Early on Tuesday morning my brother called with the news that our mother had died. Mom was eighty-one years old, had been in poor health, and had suffered from a form of Alzheimer's disease for several years. Although she had been declining, the timing of her death was a surprise. Like so many people before me, I can testify that even if you expect it, you're never really ready for the death of a parent. It hits you harder than you expect. So we rounded up the boys and began making the trip to Alabama for the funeral service. I was still sick and couldn't drive. So they laid me in the backseat, and the boys and Marlene took turns driving. The next night we had the visitation, and I saw lots of family friends I hadn't seen for almost three decades.

The day after that I spoke at the graveside service. It was cold and a bit windy on that early March day when we laid my mother to rest next to my father who had died twenty-nine years earlier. Over a hundred people gathered for the brief service. The thought occurred to me that I hadn't seen most of these people since my father's funeral in 1974. My high school principal was there, folks from the church where we grew up were there, as were many old family friends who had known my father and mother many years ago.

While I was standing there doing my mother's graveside service, I had a surreal personal experience. Perhaps it happened partly because of my sickness, perhaps it was seeing so many old friends after three decades, perhaps it was because we were burying my mother and my father side by side. It was as if there was a "wrinkle in time" and the twenty-nine years since my father died had suddenly been swallowed up. They just disappeared for a moment. I was in my early twenties when Dad died; I'm in my early fifties now. Most of the family friends who came to the graveside service had been at my father's funeral twenty-nine years earlier. Most of them were in their early fifties then; most are in their late seventies or early eighties now. It seemed as if the three decades in between had just disappeared.

All this passed through my mind in a flash while I was speaking. I could reach out and touch my mother's coffin. I was standing three feet from where we'd buried my father. It was as if we had buried my father just the week before, we were burying my mother this week, and next week someone would bury me. I had a tremendous sense of my own mortality, of the quickly passing years. It seemed as if the Lord whispered in my ear, "Ray, take a good look. This is where you will be someday." And that day comes sooner than we think.

Yesterday my father died.

Today my mother died.

Tomorrow I will die.

Decades may pass between those events. But all are certain to happen. I cannot totally explain what I experienced that day; yet it was profound to me, and I am still thinking about it. The sickness and my mother's death were a revelation of my own weakness, my humanity, my frailty, a reminder that "dust thou art, and unto dust shalt thou return" (Genesis 3:19, KJV). This is always true for all of us, but often we live as if we don't believe it.

As I survey my own life a year and a half later, I find a huge desire to simplify things. I have spoken about this before because it is a compelling urge inside me. Simplify. Find out what really matters. Don't carry so much clutter. Get rid of what you don't need. Pack the essentials, and don't worry about anything else. And above all, trust in a sovereign God. This doctrine has become my bedrock. I can live without many things, but I cannot live without a sovereign God. And I find a new desire to know God in all that I do. While meditating on 1 Peter 1:16 ("You shall be holy, for I am holy"), it occurred to me that holiness remains a mystery for most believers. We know what the word means, but we have a hard time explaining what it looks like. So here's another interpretation. God says, "Be like me." That's right—God wants us to be like him. Holiness is the essence of who God is, and God says, "Be like me."

- In your going and coming, be like me.
- In your buying and selling, be like me.
- In your sleeping and waking, be like me.
- In your thinking and dreaming, be like me.
- In your words and deeds, be like me.
- In all parts of your life, be like me.

Talk about raising the bar! That's a high standard. It goes far beyond the usual list of dos and don'ts that we associate with being holy. Many people think holiness is boring and stuffy, but that's because they associate it with a rulebook. But that's not how the Bible presents it. *Being holy is being like God. And that's the most exciting thing in the world.* Holiness means being so much like God that you change the world. Or to be more precise, holiness means being so much like God that the world begins to change around you.

If you doubt my words, would you accept the words of C. S. Lewis? This is what Lewis said about holiness:

> How little people know who think that holiness is dull. When one meets the real thing . . . it is irresistible. If even ten percent of the world's population had it, would not the whole world be converted and happy before a year's end? (*Letters to an American Lady* [Grand Rapids, MI: Eerdmans, 1967], p. 28)

He's right. People who think holiness is dull don't understand what it really means. *When you meet truly holy persons, you feel drawn to them because they are so much like God.* We've all known at least one person like that—someone whose life radiates God in such a way that you were drawn to him or her. Almost always such people are filled with a kind of contagious joy. They are like God—and they are filled with joy! What a fantastic combination. That's what the Bible means when it speaks of "the beauty of holiness" (1 Chronicles 16:29, KJV; ESV: "the splendor of holiness"). Holy people have holy joy. *They enjoy life because they are full of God.* Maybe we aren't enough like God, and so we are easily resistible. If Lewis is right, if only 10 percent of us had this sort of holy joy, we'd see whole cities converted by the end of the year. Maybe the people around us have seen us and our religion, but they haven't seen enough of God in us, and not that much joy.

God says, "Be like me." Holiness is not a set of rules and regulations. Holiness is about God!

- God when I wake up.
- God in the shower.
- God around the breakfast table.
- God on the way to work.
- God in the classroom.
- God in the showroom.
- God in the office.
- God in the factory.
- God at lunchtime.
- God during break.
- God on the way home.
- God at the supper table.
- God while watching TV.
- God while reading e-mail.
- God while surfing the Internet.
- God on the telephone.
- God at bedtime.
- God while I sleep.
- God in the morning all over again.
- God in every detail.
- God in every place.
- God always and forever.
- God under my feet.
- God all around me.
- God in my deepest thoughts.
- God in every relationship.
- God in every word.
- God in every thought.
- God in every deed.
- God in my private moments.
- God with my friends.
- God with my enemies.
- God when I am happy.
- God when I am sad.
- God in the good times.
- God in the bad times.
- God in my faith.
- God in my doubts.
- God when I succeed.
- God in my failures.
- God above me.
- God below me.
- God before me.
- God behind me.
- God around me.
- God within me.
- God first and last.
- God above my head.
- God guiding all I do and say.

Always God, always there, always with me, now and forever. This is true holiness. This is true joy. *This is the purpose for which I was created.* And without God, I have no meaning, no purpose, and no reason for being here.

Moses received his answer, but not in the way he expected. And it did not come without a revelation of his own weakness. The same is true for all of us. We say we want to know the Lord better, we want to come closer to him in prayer, we want to grow in grace, we hope to move forward in our spiritual journey. *But there is a price to be paid.* No pain, no gain. We must see our own weakness in a personal way before we can behold his glory.

Truth #3:
When this prayer is answered,
others will know it before you will

Exodus 34:29 tells us that when Moses came down from the mountain, his face was radiant because he had been speaking with God, but he didn't know it. He had been with God so long that some of God's glory rubbed off on him. The people saw his shining face and knew that he had been with God. Moses had no idea his face was shining until they told him. Evidently it was too much to look at; so he veiled his face so he wouldn't blind his friends.

Sometimes we pray, "Lord, show me your glory," hoping for some deep personal experience that will transform us on the inside. Although we wouldn't say it this way, we secretly hope that by drawing close to God, we will have some experience that will make us better people, banish our doubts, increase our faith, free us from temptation, and fill our hearts with joy. In short, we want to know God better for our own benefit. But in Moses' case, the real benefit was seen by others. They saw the visible evidence of God's work before he did.

Occasionally I'm in a meeting where someone will ask, "Are you closer to the Lord today than you were a year ago?" I never know how to answer that question in a satisfactory manner. I certainly hope that I am closer to the Lord today than I was a year ago, but my judgment is necessarily flawed because I don't see myself clearly. I see what I want to see, or I see what I would like to see. Sometimes I look at my life and feel there has been no progress at all. The best way to answer a question like this is to ask the people who know me best. My wife, my boys, the people I work with every day—they know the truth about me. If I have been walking with the Lord, others will know it; they will see the light shining from me even when I'm not aware of it.

So do not be dismayed if you feel that you have made little progress spiritually. *No matter how far we come, there is always more ground to cover for the Lord.* And often when we think we're going in circles, we are actually ascending the mountain of the Lord. Sometimes it takes a friend who can say, "Look how far you've come. I can see God's work in your life." That was true for Moses. It will be true for us as well.

There is great encouragement for all of us from this ancient story. In a time of crisis Moses dared to pray a magnificent prayer to the Lord. He asked for more than any man had asked for before, and he received more than any man had ever received. Yet both the prayer and the answer came in a time of crisis through a revelation of Moses' own weakness. And the answer was seen by others before it was seen by Moses. These things are here for our encouragement. Your trials are not meant to destroy you. God intends that you should use the hard times to draw near to him. If you are willing to be made weak, you will learn things about the Lord that you never knew when you were strong. This is always God's way. The strong have no need of God—or so they think. But the weak are hidden in a cleft of the rock—and they are the ones who truly see God.

QUESTIONS FOR PERSONAL/GROUP STUDY

1. Why is God's glory more often seen at our crisis points than when things are going well?

2. What are some ways God's glory is seen in our lives? Why is it important to review those experiences?

3. Are you closer to the Lord today than you were a year ago? Why is it often difficult to answer that question?

4. What things in your life make you hesitant to pray, "Lord,

show me your glory"? Are there areas in your life that are closed to God's influence?

5. Why did God tell Moses he could not show him all his glory? What about God's glory is too awesome for us to handle?

6. Do you agree that holiness is the most exciting thing in the world? What difference would it make if you were more like God every day?

GOING DEEPER

Ask your husband, wife, brother, sister, or trusted friend if they have seen evidence of spiritual growth in your life. Ponder their answers, and ask God to reveal areas in your life that need changing so his glory can be seen. As God reveals these things, write them down and for the next month pray for daily growth in those areas.

OVERCOMING FEAR OF THE FUTURE

Current headlines tell a chilling story, often making us uncertain and fearful of what is going on or might happen in our world.

> More Unrest in the Middle East
> Riots Erupt in Indonesia
> The High Cost of Peace
> New Security Measures for Air Travelers
> Terrorism on the High Seas
> Iran Prepares for War
> Predictions for Perilous Times

The last headline is arresting, at least for those of us raised on the King James Bible, because it calls to mind a verse many of us heard (and memorized) years ago: "In the last days perilous times shall come" (2 Timothy 3:1). These are indeed "perilous times" in many ways. Columnist George Will suggests that we live in a period of history more dangerous than anything the world has known in the last seven centuries ("Danger in the New Year," January 1, 2003). He frames the issue in these stark terms:

The clash between science and religion was supposed to be a defining characteristic of the modern age. But today's distinctive terror is modern science in the service of religious fanatics—or, in North Korea, of fanatics drunk on the dregs of the pseudo religion of scientific socialism imagined by a 19th-century German exile toiling in the British Museum. Talk about globalization.

The danger of all-out war in the Middle East, the saber-rattling by various nations, and the continuing threat of bioterrorism combine to make this a dangerous time to be alive, or more accurately, a dangerous time to try to stay alive.

And yet life goes on—a bit uncertainly perhaps, but we all have our business to attend to. There are classes to teach, orders to fill, patients to see, books to write (and read), games to be played (and watched), papers to write, bills to pay, medicine to take, songs to sing, meals to prepare, and beyond that, the closer concerns of marriage and children and friends and family members. Many days it is easier to dismiss the larger concerns of the world in favor of wondering how you will spend Saturday night.

At the end of a recent sermon I invited people to write down their three biggest worries, concerns, or fears and then come forward to put them in a "Worry Box," signifying that they were giving those things to the Lord in an act of faith and surrender to him. A brief survey reveals that the concerns of the congregation are universal. The very first one I pulled out at random (the cards are unsigned) says simply, "Financial security. Health. Marriage." Another lists "A place to live." Another adds, "Walk with God. Loneliness." Another says simply, "School." One reads: "Healthy family. Money. Faith in God." A few others include: "Dad's salvation." "Unable to get pregnant." "Anxiety level." "I'm afraid I won't serve the Lord." "Future family???" "Job loss." Who among us could not relate to these concerns? I did find several that mentioned the world situation. One simply said, "War, of course." They are not unaware of what is happening in the world, but their deepest worries are closer to home.

Someone has said that worry is "the interest paid by those who borrow trouble." Another person called worry "a thin stream of fear trickling through the mind." According to John Haggai, "In America, worry has become part of our national culture. You could write on countless American gravestones the epitaph: 'Hurried, Worried, Buried.'"

Perhaps our greatest fear is the fear of death. Hebrews 2:15 tells us that Christ came to deliver those who had been enslaved by the fear of death all their lives. It's not just the fear of dying that troubles us; it's the thought of leaving this life with so much left to do. *For some people both living and dying can seem equally painful.* How can we overcome our fear over what might happen to us in the future? With all that looms before us, both internationally and personally, how can we move from fear to faith? In order to answer those questions, let's take a look at the story of a young woman named Esther. Even though the events took place almost twenty-five centuries ago, the story of her amazing courage points the way to a life free from consuming fear over what might happen tomorrow.

A MAN CALLED XERXES

The year was 465 B.C. A man named Xerxes (also called Ahasuerus) was the king of Persia. The most powerful man in the world, he ruled an empire even bigger than the earlier Babylonian empire of Nebuchadnezzar. His empire spread from India in the east to Greece in the west to Africa in the south to Turkey in the north. Our story takes place in one of his capital cities. In those days the Persian Empire had four capital cities. One you've heard of—Babylon. Another one was called Ecbatana. Another was called Persepolis. And yet a fourth one was called Susa. It is in Susa that our story unfolds.

It is fitting that we should consider a story that took place in Susa, for it is not far from the center of action in the Middle East today. In fact, archaeologists dug up Susa about a hundred years ago and found the ruins of the palace spoken of in the book of Esther. If you want to get to Susa, you could fly into Baghdad, take a bus out of the city, and go south toward the mouth of the Persian Gulf. When you get to the mouth of the Persian Gulf you would turn left across the coastlands, cross the disputed border with Iran, and then make your way for another hundred miles. You would begin to come north again into the Plain of Khuzistan, and there, by the shores of the Karkheh River, you would see what would appear to be a large mound, flat on top, with some ruins above it. That is all that is left today of the ancient city of Susa.

The King's Winter Palace

But in 465 B.C. Susa was one of the world's greatest cities. Darius the Mede, father of King Xerxes, had built his winter palace there. Archaeologists discovered a tablet in the ruins that describes how that king built the city of Susa. Darius imported cedar from Lebanon, hard wood from Gandara, gold from Sardis, lapis lazuli from Sogdiana, ebony and silver from Egypt, ivory from Ethiopia, and turquoise from Chorasmia. After he died, Xerxes continued the work his father had begun. The real capital was in Babylon. Susa, home of the winter palace, was a place to get away from the pressures of Babylon.

The king of Persia kept his harem in Susa, a large group of beautiful women who were at his beck and call to serve him in any way he wished. They were gathered from among the most beautiful women in the empire—both Persian women and women from foreign countries. They had been given a special diet and were taught a special way of life, and their only calling was to please the king. One after another he would call the women in, and they would serve him and do his bidding.

HOW A JEWISH PRINCESS BECAME A QUEEN

In the course of time the king, who had become enraged at Queen Vashti for some (in his mind) indiscretions, began to search his harem for the most beautiful, most attractive, most desirable woman, so that he might make her the new queen. He looked at one woman after another, but he could not find what he wanted—until at last he came upon a woman whose beauty, character, form, and comeliness was such that he was completely taken with her. He said, "I want her to be my queen." Her name in Hebrew was Hadassah and in Persian Esther. She was a Jew. This member of God's chosen people, without any forewarning, suddenly became the Queen of Persia. She was now the most important woman in the entire realm. A Jewish woman was now queen to a Persian king!

Life was good for Esther because she was the king's chosen one. She was the one on whom his favor rested. For many days, months, and years Esther basked in the glory of being the chief woman of the realm, the one to whom everyone else bowed and paid homage.

WICKED HAMAN

It came to pass that a certain man named Haman came in to see the king. Esther knew nothing about it because in those days the king kept his business and his women far apart. So while Esther was with the other women, the king spoke with Haman. That man came in with a story the king could hardly believe. "Your Majesty, there is a certain people in your realm who are treasonous and seditious against you. They do not follow your law. They do not pay homage to you. They do not respect what you have done. We must do something about these people." Haman neglected to tell the king that he was talking about the Jews. As a matter of fact, the things he was saying were not true. The Jews were not seditious; they were not treasonous. But Haman, because he was a descendant of the Amalekites, the ancient enemies of the people of God, wanted to stir up trouble against the Jews.

So he said to the king, "We must do something about these people who are polluting your kingdom." The king asked, "What do you propose?" And Haman answered, "If you will allow me, I will write a decree and have you sign it with your signet ring, and we will send a decree throughout the Kingdom. The decree will be that on a certain day all these people will be put to death." This is called a pogrom. It is an ancient version of what the Nazis did in World War II. Haman's idea was to kill all the Jews in the Persian Empire on the same day. Again, Haman neglected to tell the king that he was talking about the Jews; the king didn't know—not that it would have made that much difference to a Persian king anyway. So the decree was signed and sealed with the monarch's signet ring, and it began to go out over all the land.

SACKCLOTH AND ASHES

Enter a man by the name of Mordecai, cousin to Queen Esther. He was a Jew serving in the court of King Xerxes. He was involved in the business affairs of the king, a man of good character, a man whom the king greatly respected. When Mordecai heard what wicked Haman had done, which would mean that he and all his relatives would be put to death, he went to the middle of the city, clothed himself with sackcloth and ashes, and began mourning and wailing.

Word of what Mordecai had done reached the ears of Queen Esther. She had not heard about Haman's wicked plot, and when she heard that Mordecai was in mourning, she sent her messenger to find out what had happened. He gave the messenger a copy of the decree and said, "Go back to the queen, and tell her that she is the only one who can save us now. If she does not act, we will all die."

DON'T CALL ME, I'LL CALL YOU

We pick up the story in Esther 4:9-11.

> *And Hathach [the messenger from Esther] went and told Esther what Mordecai had said. Then Esther spoke to Hathach and commanded him to go to Mordecai and say, "All the king's servants and the people of the king's provinces know that if any man or woman goes to the king inside the inner court without being called, there is but one law—to be put to death."*

All the monarchs of the ancient Near East were absolute despots. You could not come near them without an invitation. If a man rushed in to see the king and the king was startled and didn't want to see him, without a word the man would be taken out and put to death. So you had to think and think again before you went in to see the king. The only exception was "the one to whom the king holds out the golden scepter so that he may live. But as for me," Esther went on, "I have not been called to come in to the king these thirty days" (v. 11b). It's hard for us to understand that today, but you must remember this was an ancient Near East nation—even though she was the queen, she was still part of the harem. The king had not seen Esther for thirty days.

COUNTING THE COST

Mordecai was saying, "Esther, you have to save us." And Esther was saying, "Mordecai, you don't understand what you're asking me to do." She wasn't refusing, you understand. She wasn't saying, "No, I won't do it." She was just saying, "Before you ask me to do that, you have to understand what the risk is. If I go in there and the king doesn't want to see me, I will be put to death even though I am the queen. Mordecai, think about what you are asking me to do." She wasn't saying no. She was doing what any reasonable individual would do. She was counting the personal cost.

That's true anytime you're called to get involved. Anytime the phone rings, anytime there's an appeal, anytime there's a great cause put before you, anytime the challenge is great, you have to consider what is involved. *Before you take the first step you had better sit down and count the personal cost.* That's a biblical thing to do. Nobody goes to war without counting the soldiers to make sure he has enough. Nobody sits down to build a building without making sure he has enough money to finish the job. If you want to be my disciple, Jesus said, you must take up your cross and follow me. It's going to cost you something (see Luke 14:27-33).

So Esther was saying, "Mordecai, I want to help you, but you have to understand something—I'm taking my life in my hands if I get involved in this." She was the queen. She had a good life. She could have anything she wanted. She would raise her hand and fifty servants would come to her. She could just say the word and it was given to her. All those other women would have given anything to be in her position. She had it all—material wealth, fame, popularity, adulation, the approval of her friends. Now Mordecai was saying, "Esther, it's time for you to put it all on the line."

NO ESCAPE

The messenger went back and told Mordecai what Esther had said. Mordecai's answer is the heart of the book of Esther:

> *Then Mordecai told them to reply to Esther, "Do not think to yourself that in the king's palace you will escape any more than all the other Jews. For if you keep silent at this time, relief and deliverance will rise for the Jews from another place, but you and your father's house will perish. And who knows whether*

you have not come to the kingdom for such a time as this?"
(4:13-14)

He made three appeals to her. *The first one was the lowest-level appeal.* He said in essence, "Esther, you're the queen, but underneath all that queenly regalia beats a Jewish heart. You're one of God's people. Don't think by remaining silent you can avoid persecution, because you can't. Once the killing starts, it's going to be mighty hard to stop. Once the crowds start killing the Jews one by one, they'll start with the common people; but, Esther, they'll wind up on your doorstep, and they won't stop killing until they've killed *all* the Jews, including you and your family. Don't think that your position or privilege exempts you from what is going to happen. Just because you're the queen, you are not out of trouble. You may be the last to go, but you're going to go."

We should learn from this that there is no safety in this world, not even for the rich and powerful. After 9/11 we ought to be fully convinced of this fact. Riches cannot save us from the troubles of the world.

THE UNNAMED GOD

Then he said, "If you keep silent at this time, relief and deliverance will rise for the Jews from another place." This is one of the most amazing statements in all of the Old Testament. It is certainly the most amazing statement in the book of Esther. By the way, let me share a piece of Bible trivia with you. Did you know that Esther is the only book in the Bible in which the name of God is not mentioned? You will never find the words *God* or *Lord* in the book of Esther. That's one of the reasons some people have looked at that book and have concluded that it's not important or not inspired or doesn't belong in the Bible or isn't worthy of our close study. But I'll tell you why the name of God is not in there. It's because the book of Esther is the story of God's people in a foreign land. It's the story of God's people under Gentile domination. It is a real story that serves as a kind of parable to teach us a lesson about how God works through seemingly unconnected circumstances to deliver his people even when they are under the domination of the ungodly. That is why the name God never appears. Esther believed in God. So did Mordecai. So did all the Jews. That's what made them Jews—they believed in God. But God's name is never mentioned because it's a lesson about his providence and liberating power.

So Mordecai was saying, "If you don't help us, God is able to help us from some other source—but you yourself will be destroyed." Then he said, "Who knows whether you have not come to the kingdom for such a time as this?" Ponder those words for a moment. "Esther, don't forget where you came from. There was a time when you were lined up with all those other women in the harem. You ate at the same table with them. You dressed the same way they dress. You acted just like them. Nobody knew you were a Jew. Esther, what made the king pick you out? Did you think it was just your good looks? They were all good-looking. Do you think it was just your smile? They could all smile. Do you think it was just the way you flirted? They could all flirt."

Mordecai's message was crystal-clear: "Esther, you're the queen. You have it all. You're on top. You have privilege beyond anyone else in the whole kingdom. Do you think that happened by chance? Do you think that's coincidence? Esther, the reason you're on top is because God put you there. Do you know why God put you there? He put you there so that at this crucial moment of history you could say the word and deliver your people. All of that training and all you went through happened so that you would be the instrument God would use to deliver his people."

IF I PERISH, I PERISH

What a view of history this is. What a way of looking at the circumstances of life. What a way of understanding the work of

God. "Esther, who knows but that you have come to royal position for such a time as this?" (v. 14, NIV). For this critical moment. For this one moment in history. "Who knows, Esther, but that you have come here for this one thing? All that's happened to you is preparation for this moment."

We read Esther's response in 4:15-16:

> *Then Esther told them to reply to Mordecai, "Go, gather all the Jews to be found in Susa, and hold a fast on my behalf, and do not eat or drink for three days, night or day. I and my young women will also fast as you do. Then I will go to the king, though it is against the law, and if I perish, I perish."*

Do you get the principle here? Mordecai's great appeal to Esther was based on a great truth: *The greater the privilege, the greater the responsibility.* The more you have, the more you have to answer for. The more God has given you, the greater your responsibility to use it for his Kingdom.

What does this ancient story teach us about overcoming our own fear of the future? For one thing, we learn that *there is no safety in the world.* Bad things happen to good people all the time. Sometimes they appear to be "random" acts of tragedy, and sometimes evil people conspire against us. We also learn that *there are no coincidences in life.* You are where you are because God wants you to be there. You probably aren't a queen in a foreign court, but wherever you are right now, God had a hand in getting you there. *And your highest calling is to use your position in life to support the cause of Christ in the world.*

In the end we must do what Esther did—fast and pray and seek the Lord so that when the time comes, we can do the right thing, the hard thing, the tough choice that lies along the road of obedience to God, leaving the results with him. That's the real meaning of, "If I perish, I perish." Those are solemn words of faith spoken by a woman who has put her life in God's hands.

As I thought about her courage, the Lord put this insight on my heart: *There is no one so free as the person who is not afraid to die.* If you aren't afraid to die, then you are free to serve the Lord and do whatever he calls you to do.

I spent a few minutes with a woman in the congregation I pastor who is dying of cancer. When I asked her if she loved Jesus, with a weak voice she replied, "Yes, I do." I was told it might be the last Sunday she had the strength to come to church. The ordeal she had been through was written in the lines on her face. As we talked, I realized that before long she would be in heaven, probably in just a few days. "I don't know much about death," I told her, "but I do know this much—when the time comes that you close your eyes on earth, you will open them the very next moment in heaven. And when you take your final breath on earth, your very next breath will be in the celestial air of heaven. Don't be afraid when that time comes. The Lord himself will come to greet you. The angels of God will escort you to your new home."

Then I quoted the familiar words of the apostle Paul: "to live is Christ, and to die is gain" (Philippians 1:21). To be absent from the body is to be present with the Lord (2 Corinthians 5:8). And I reminded her of the words of Jesus to the dying thief: "Today you will be with me in Paradise" (Luke 23:43). I told my friend, "You're going to go to heaven, and when you do, you'll see Jesus face to face." Finally I reminded her of the promise of Christ himself from John 14:2-3: "In my Father's house are many rooms. If it were not so, would I have told you that I go to prepare a place for you? And if I go and prepare a place for you, I will come again and will take you to myself, that where I am you may be also."

When I finished, a tear was rolling down her cheek. Then she did something that surprised me. Although she was very weak and frail, she pulled herself up from the pew, reached over and wrapped her thin arms around my neck, and hugged me. "Don't worry about anything," I told her. "You're going to be all right because you know the Lord." I firmly believe what I said. God's people die well. If you know the Lord, you don't have to fear death. And if you don't fear death, you're truly free, and the devil has lost his greatest weapon against you.

FOUR TRUTHS FOR THE FUTURE

As we look into the future, here are four truths that ought to encourage us:

• 1. God is already there because he is the God who goes before his people.

• 2. God promises to be with you no matter what happens to you.

• 3. If you know the Lord, the worst thing that can happen is that you will go to heaven, which is also the best thing that can happen to you.

• 4. You will have all the time you need to do everything God wants you to do.

In some ways, that last point is the most important one because many of us often feel a bit rushed and harried and hurried. We feel like we're behind the eight ball before the game even begins. *No matter what else happens in the days to come, rest assured that you will have all the time, all the strength, and all the wisdom you need to do everything God wants you to do.* That principle should not be stretched to mean that you are guaranteed to accomplish all your goals or that every one of your dreams will come true. We still live in a fallen world where things break down and hardly anything works quite right. But given that limitation, we can have confidence that God will supply all that we truly need when we need it, so we can do his will.

No one can say with certainty what the future will bring. None of us knows if we will even be here twelve months (or even twelve minutes) from now. But that thought should not alarm us in any way. To all our fears the Lord says quite simply, "Fear not."

- Will things get worse? "Fear not."
- Will I lose my health? "Fear not."
- Will I get cancer? "Fear not."
- Will I keep my job? "Fear not."
- Will my loved ones struggle? "Fear not."
- Will my investments collapse? "Fear not."
- Will I run out of money this year? "Fear not."
- Will tragedy strike in my family? "Fear not."
- Will my children disappoint me? "Fear not."
- Will others ridicule my faith? "Fear not."
- Will my plans come to nothing? "Fear not."
- Will my dreams turn to ashes? "Fear not."
- Will I face death this year? "Fear not."

Any of those things might happen to us; indeed, some of them are bound to happen to us eventually. But the word of the Lord remains. "Fear not." The Lord himself is with us today, and he will be with us tomorrow. We of all people ought to be optimistic. We have a great future because we have a great God. So chin up, child of God. Stop staring in the soup. Pull those shoulders back. Put a smile on your face. Take your troubles, wrap them up, and give them all to the Lord. We'll have our share of hard times, but overriding it all is the promise of God who said, "I will never leave you nor forsake you" (Hebrews 13:5).

On Christmas Day 1939, King George VI of England gave a brief radio address to his troubled nation. England was already at war with Germany. Soon all of Europe would be plunged into the horror of brutal, unrestrained warfare. Hoping to calm the troubled hearts of his countrymen, the king offered words of encouragement as the storm clouds gathered overhead. He ended his remarks by quoting a hitherto unknown poem by Minnie Louise Haskins, "The Gate of Year." It has since become known around the world:

I said to the man who stood at the gate of the year: "Give me a light, that I may tread safely into the unknown!" And he replied: "Go out into the darkness and put your hand into the hand of God. That shall be to you better than light and safer than a known way."

What a word that is for us today. No one but God knows what the future holds. Let us do as the poet suggested and place our hands in the hand of Almighty God. And let us go out into the unknown future with confidence, knowing that if God goes with us, we need not fear the future. To walk with the Lord is the greatest of all joys, and it is indeed safer than a known way.

QUESTIONS FOR PERSONAL/GROUP STUDY

1. Pick up a newspaper and look at the headlines. What do they suggest to you about the current state of the world?

2. Esther is the only book in the Bible that doesn't mention God by name. Yet it is clearly a story about God caring for and delivering his people. As you think about this story, where can you clearly see God's hand at work?

3. Read Esther 4:12-16. How does Mordecai appeal to Esther? What is her response?

4. Are you afraid to die? Why or why not?

5. Read Luke 14:25-33. What does it cost to be a disciple of Jesus? Why is it important to count the cost before making the commitment?

6. "Your highest calling is to use your position in life to support the cause of Christ in the world." In what way are you doing that right now?

GOING DEEPER

Take a piece of paper and write down your three biggest concerns or worries. Underneath those concerns, write the words of

1 Peter 5:7: "Casting all your anxieties on him, because he cares for you." As an act of faith, take your list and put it in a box or sack or bag, then throw it away. Tell the Lord that you want to place your worries in his hands.

If you would like to contact the author, you can reach him in the following ways:

BY LETTER:
Ray Pritchard
Calvary Memorial Church
931 Lake Street
Oak Park, IL 60301

BY E-MAIL:
PastorRay@calvarymemorial.com

VIA THE INTERNET:
www.keepbelieving.com